Real World Colouring Book

For Advanced Users & Adults

50 Images

Created From Real Life Photos For You To Colour As You Please.

ISBN 978-0-359-83284-2

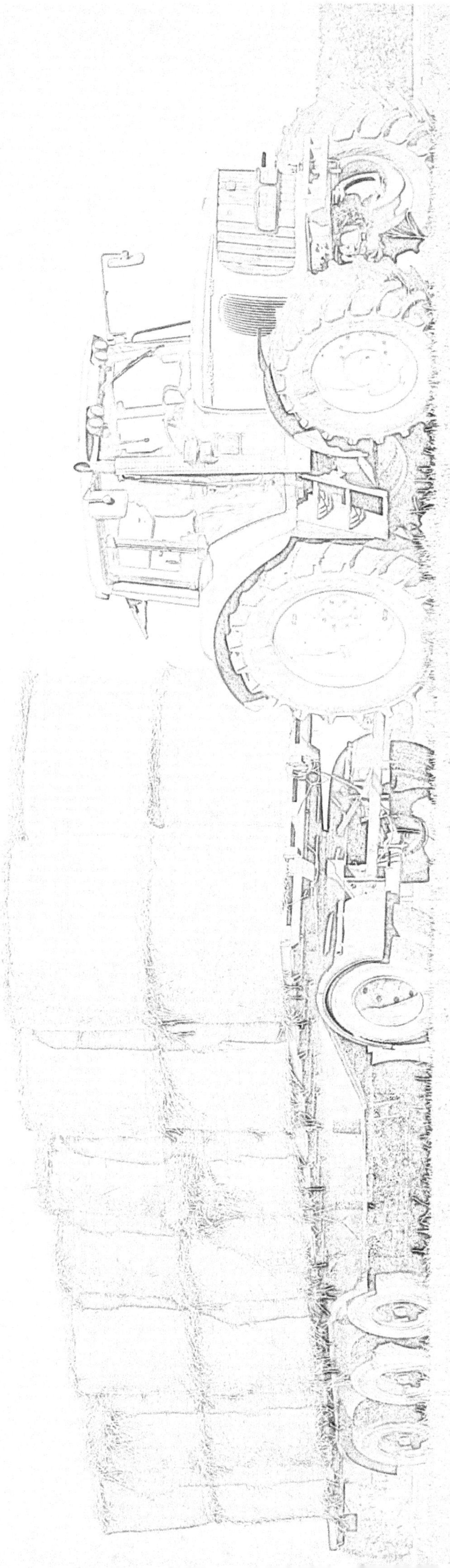

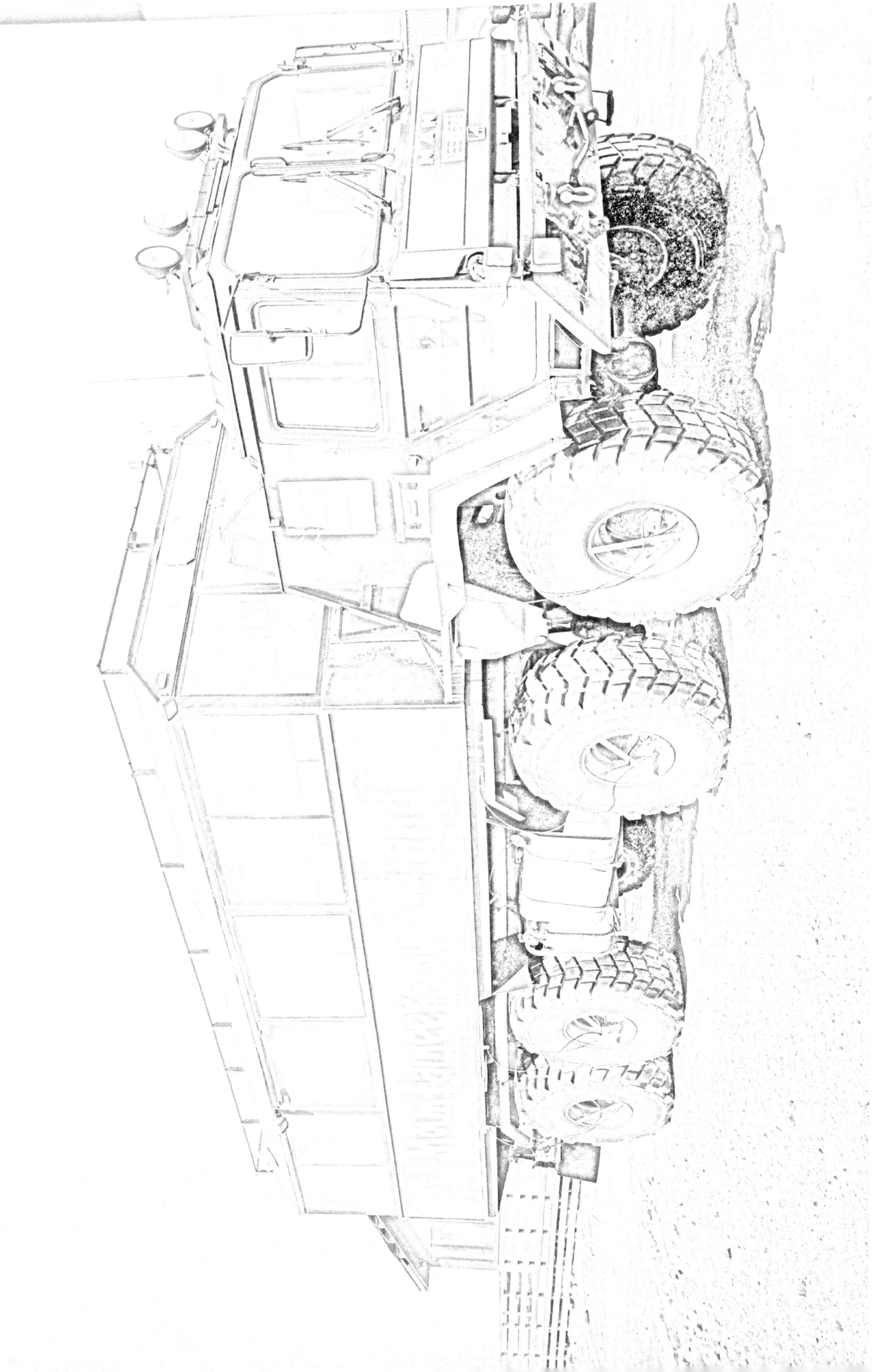

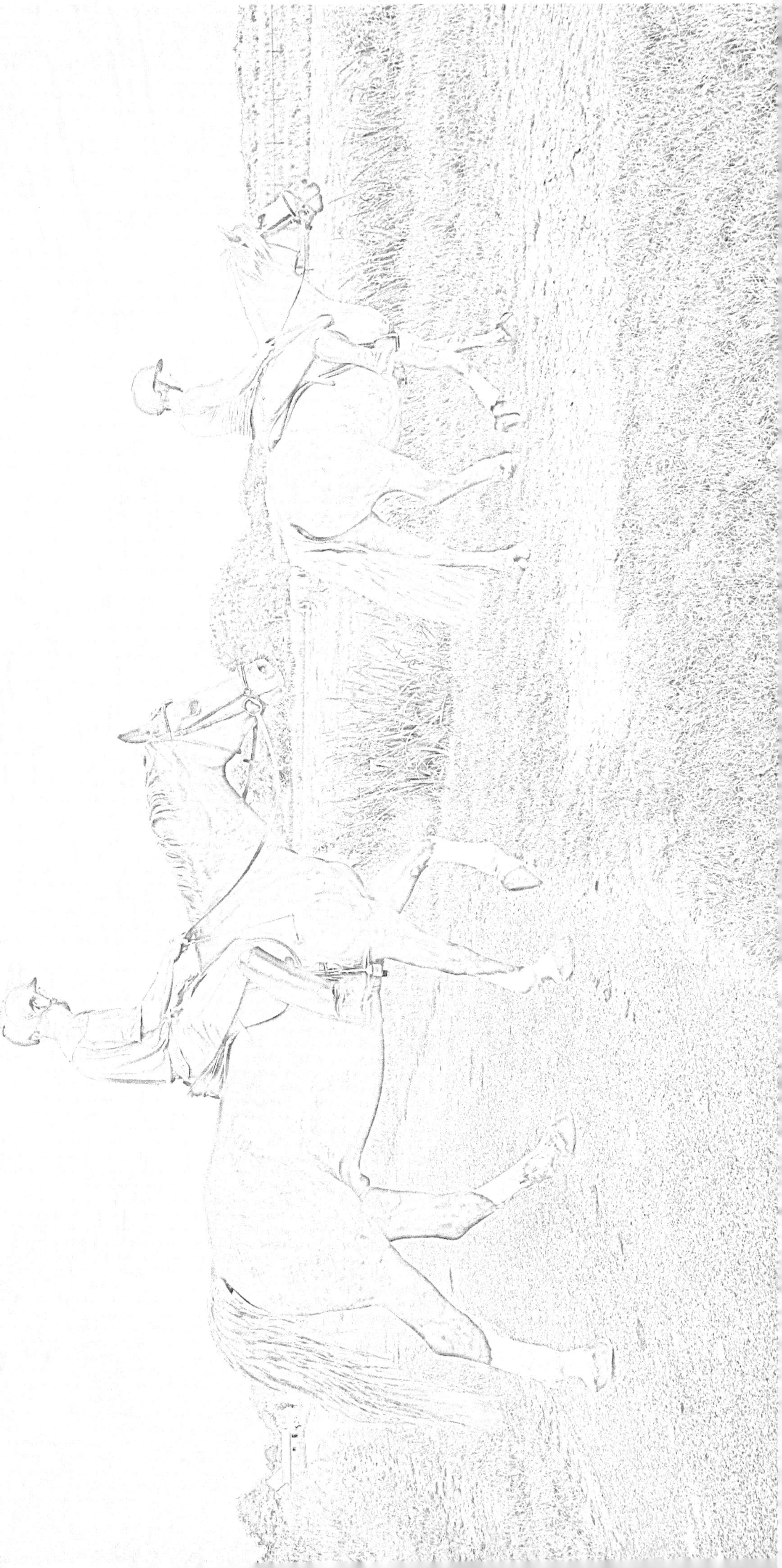

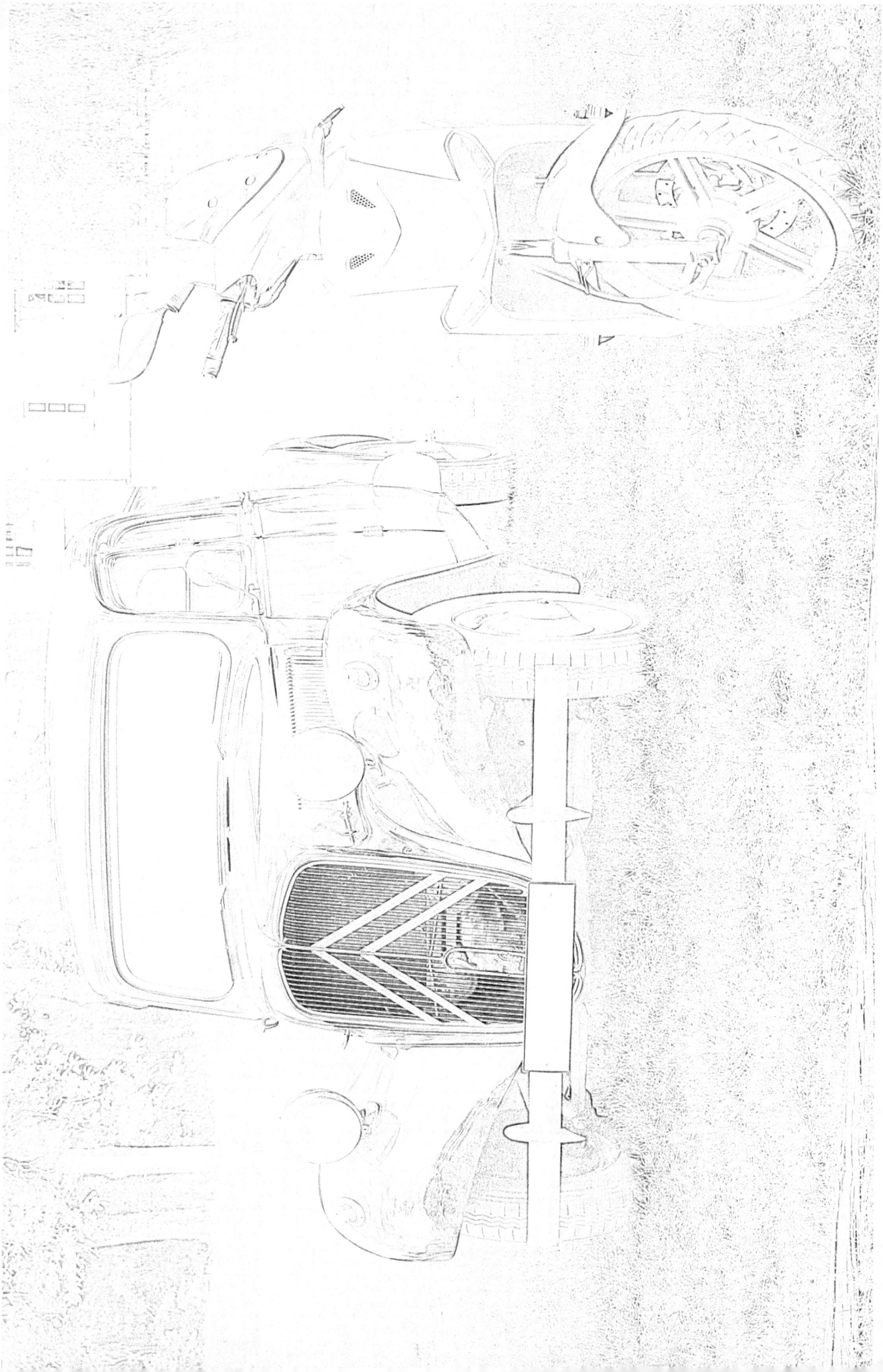

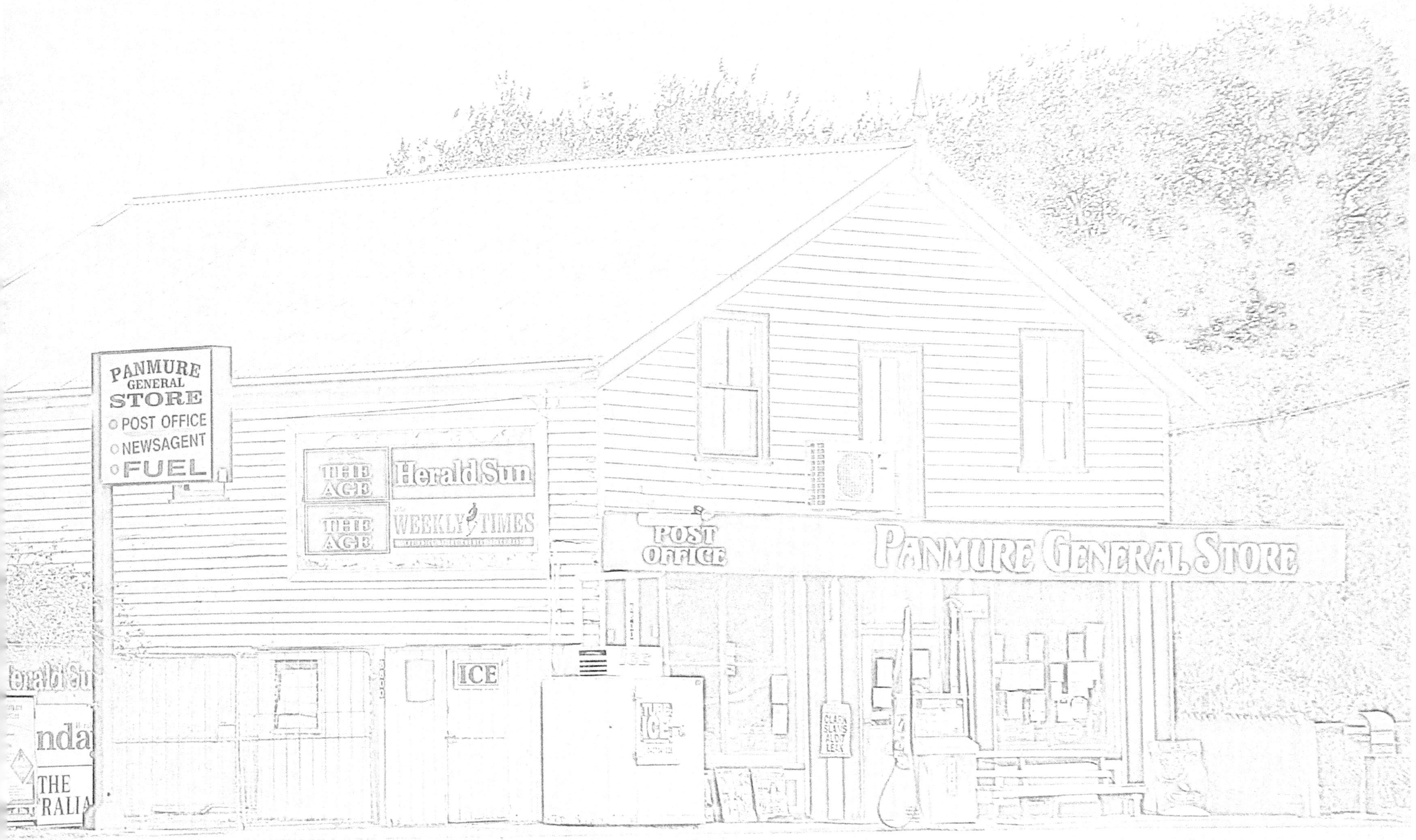
PANMURE
GENERAL
STORE
POST OFFICE
NEWSAGENT
FUEL
THE AGE
Herald Sun
THE AGE
WEEKLY TIMES
POST
OFFICE
PANMURE GENERAL STORE
ICE
THE
RALIA

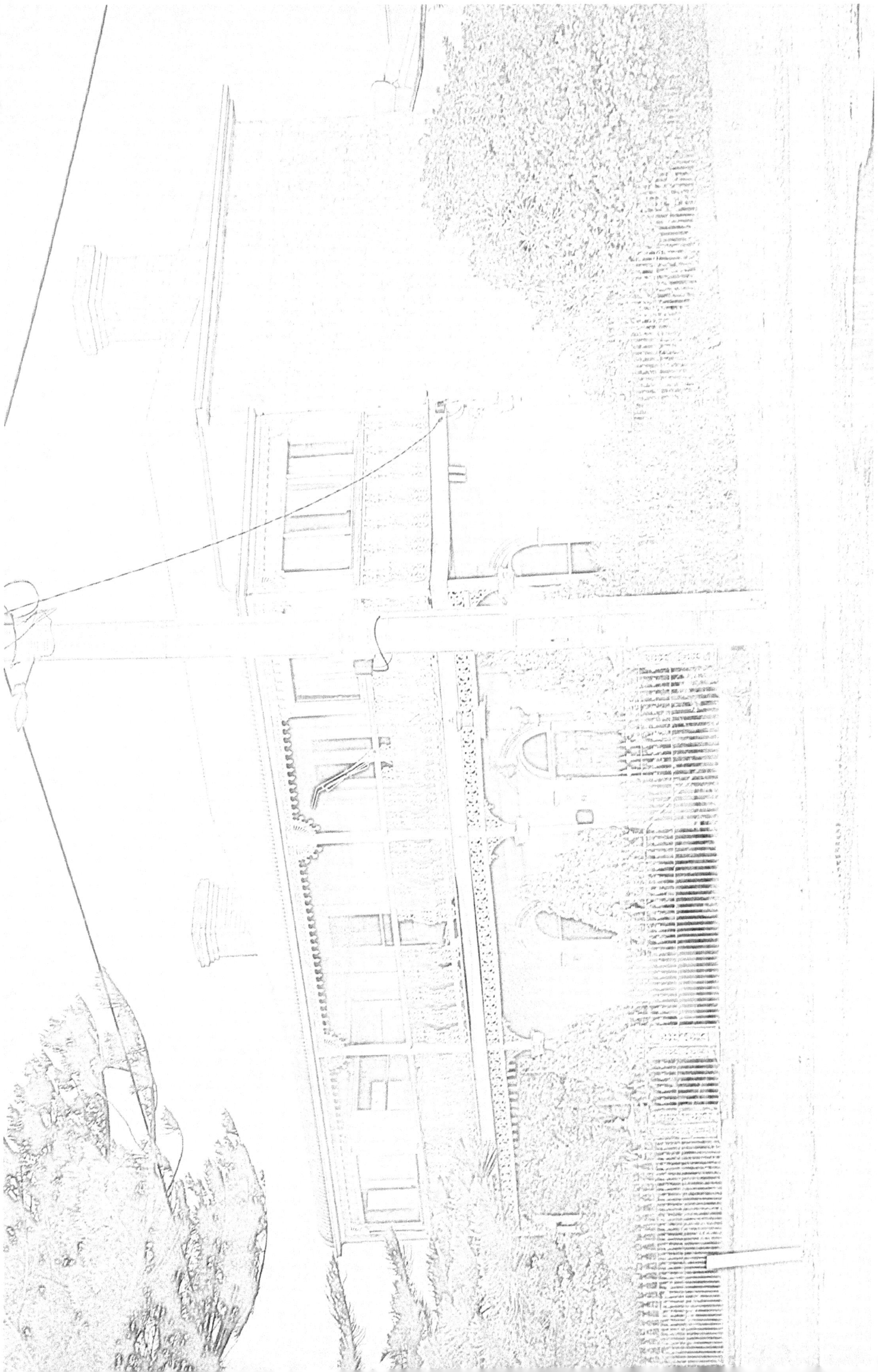

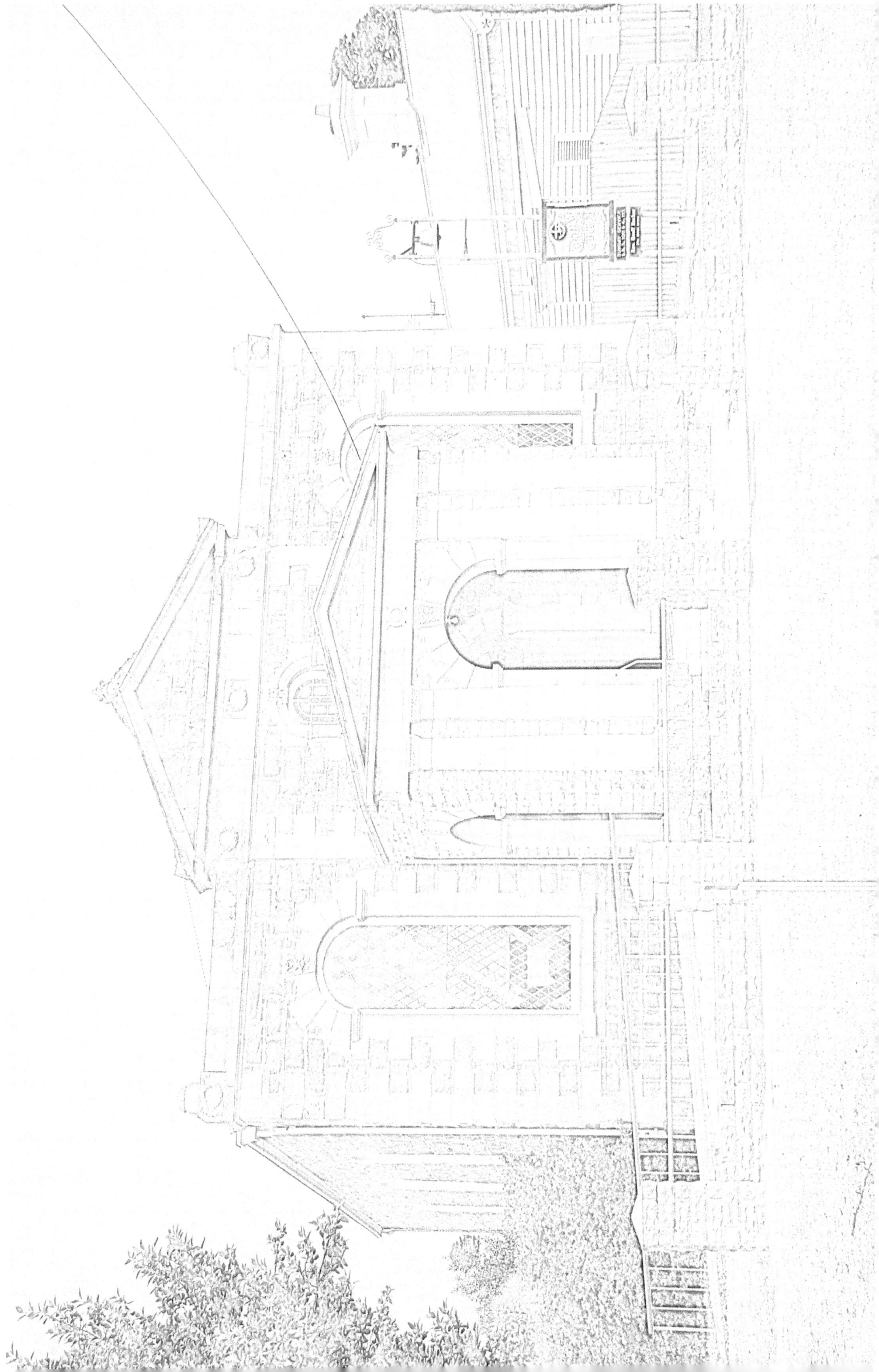

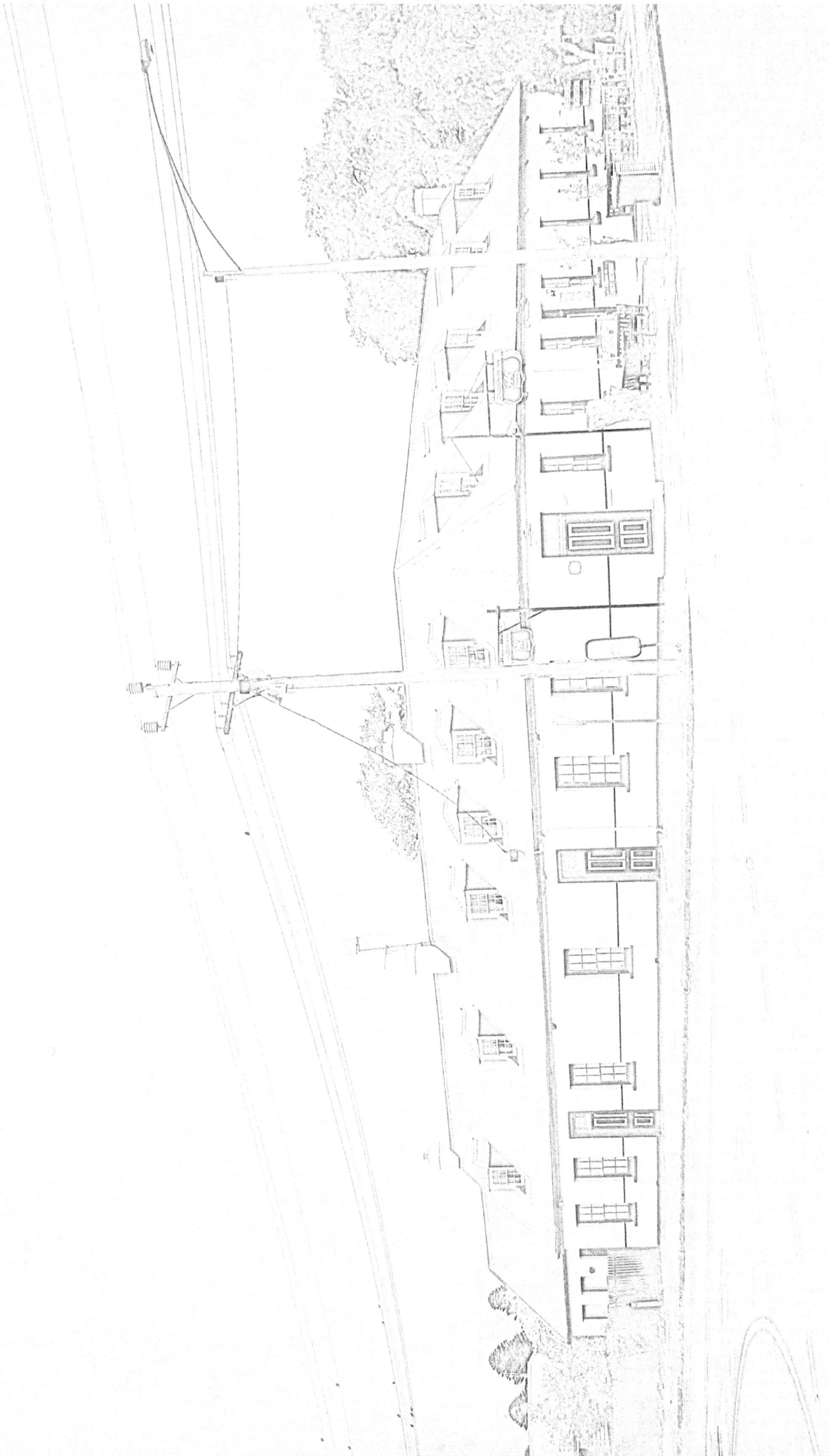

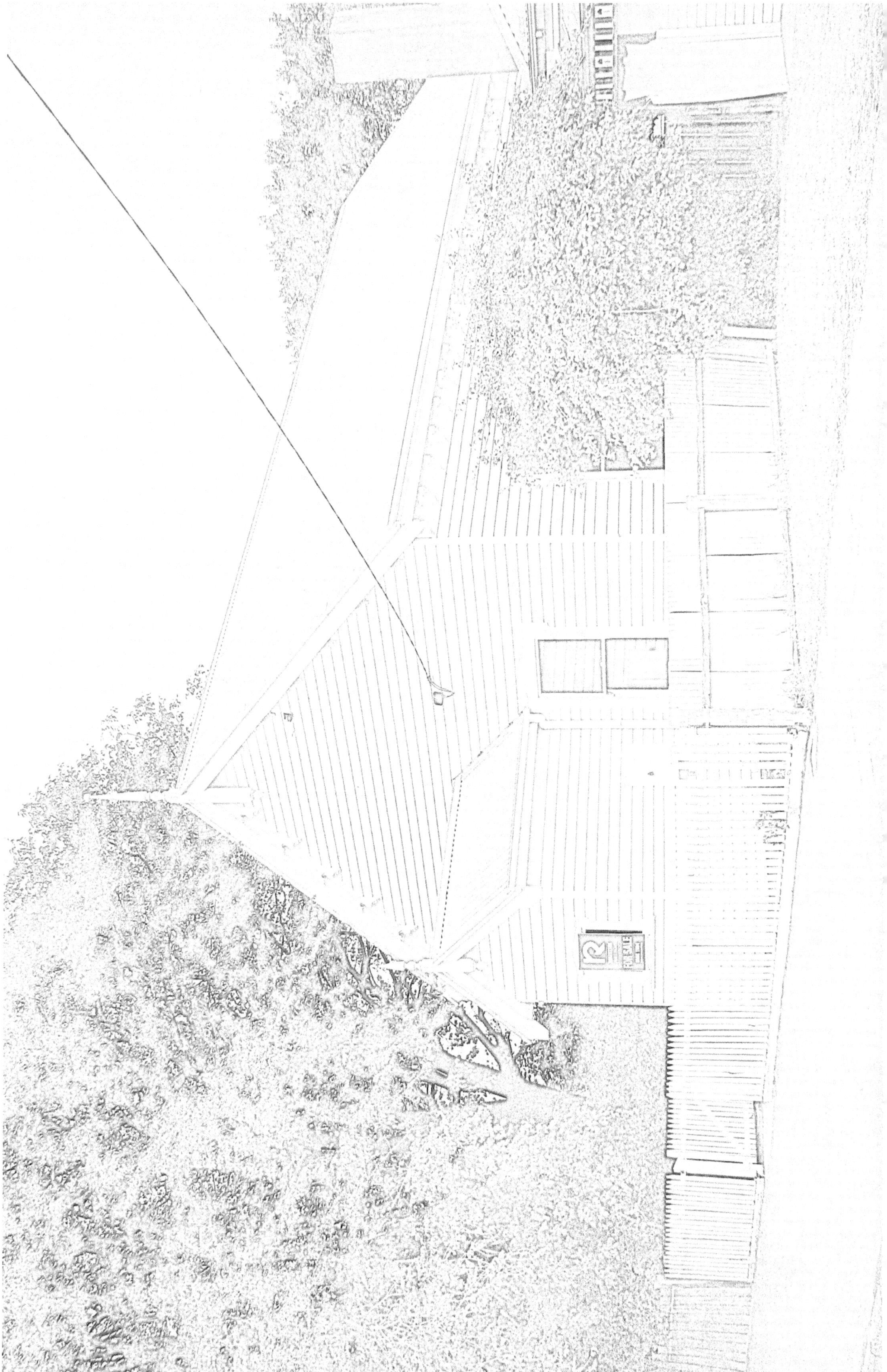

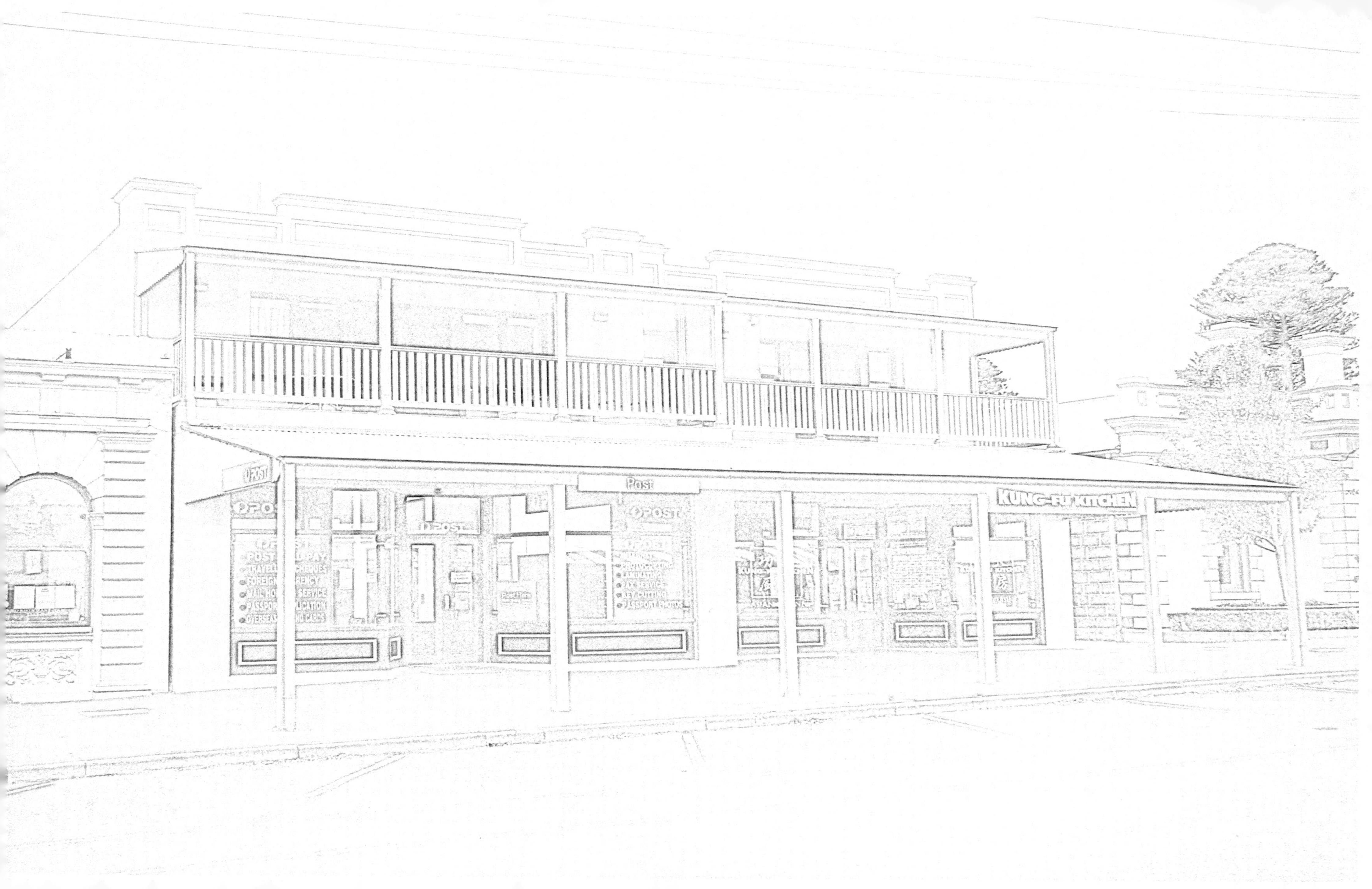

Post
KUNG-FU KITCHEN
POST
PHOTOCOPYING
LAMINATING
FAX SERVICE
KEY CUTTING
PASSPORT PHOTOS

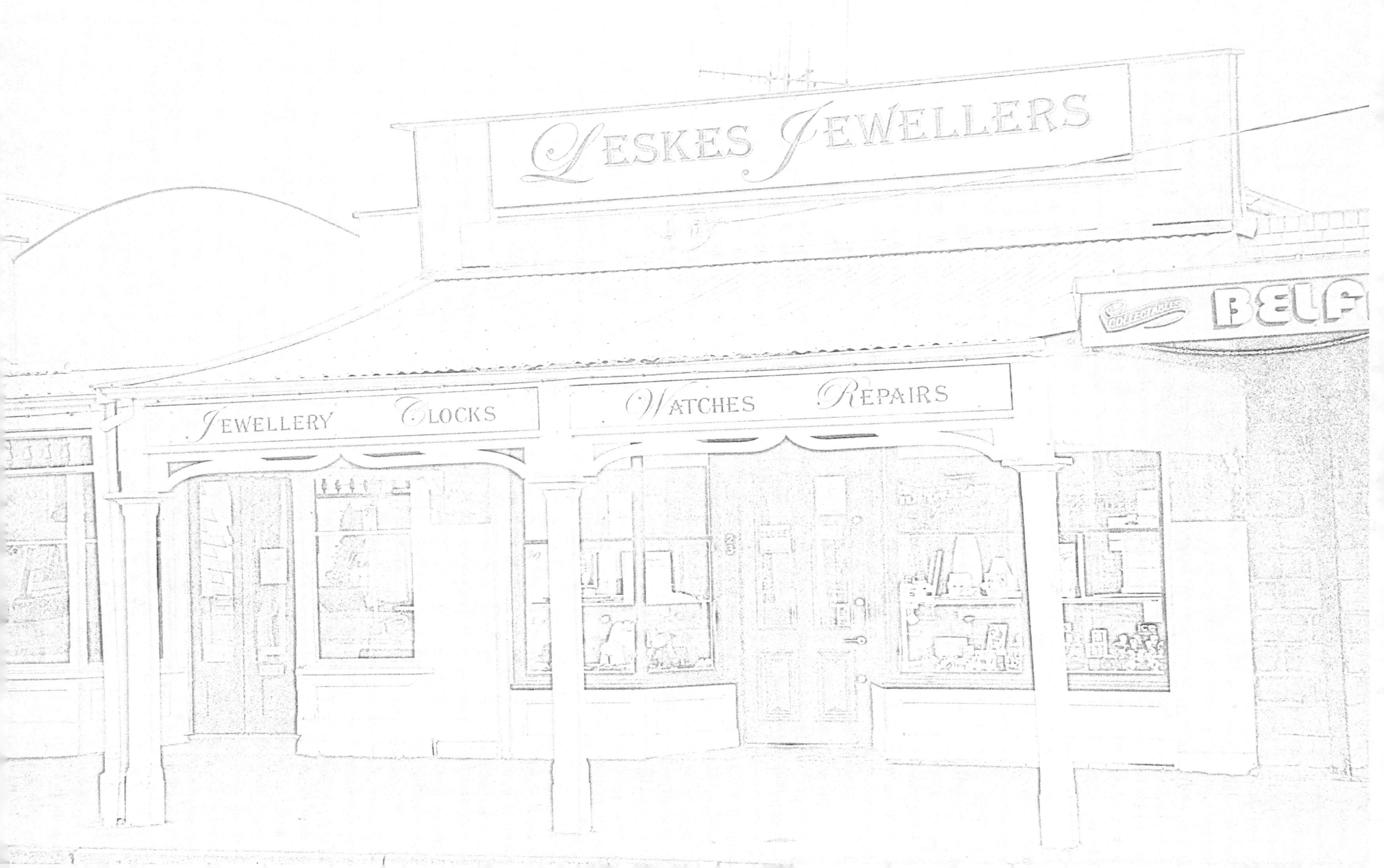
LESKES JEWELLERS
JEWELLERY
CLOCKS
WATCHES
REPAIRS
COLLECTABLES
BELG

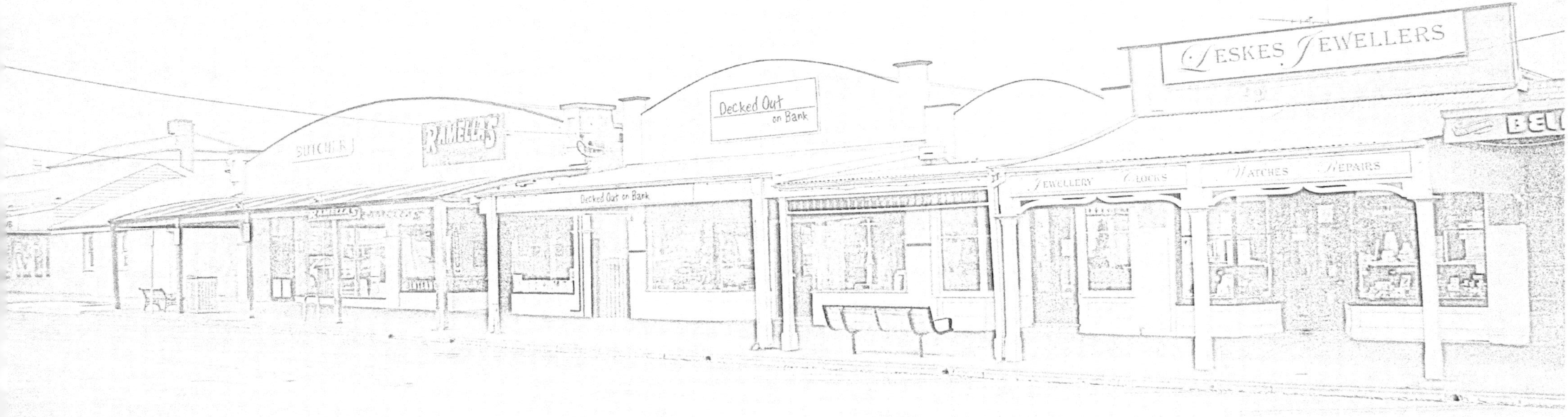
LESKES JEWELLERS
JEWELLERY CLOCKS
WATCHES REPAIRS
Decked Out on Bank
Decked Out on Bank
BUTCHER
RAMELLAS

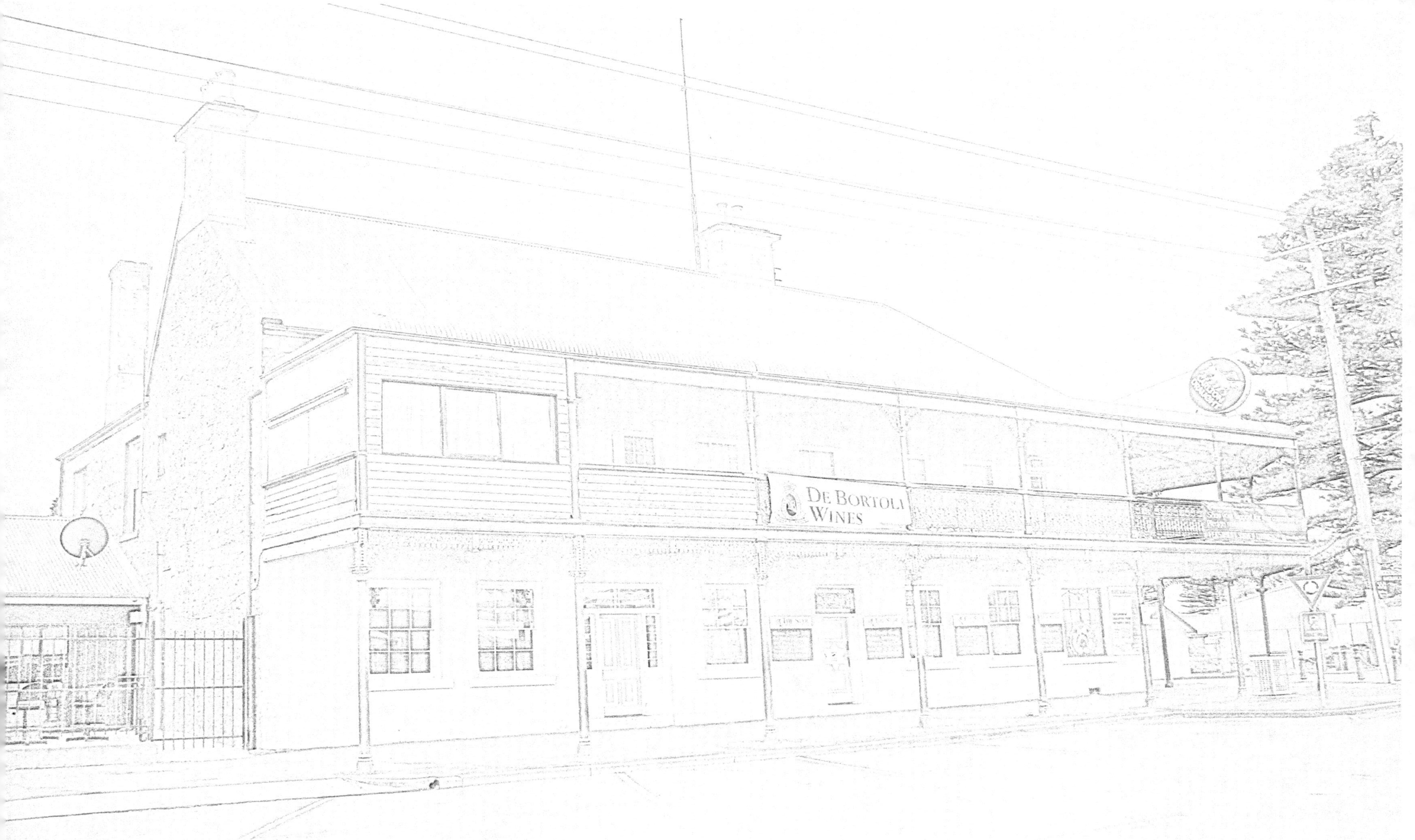
De Bortoli
Wines

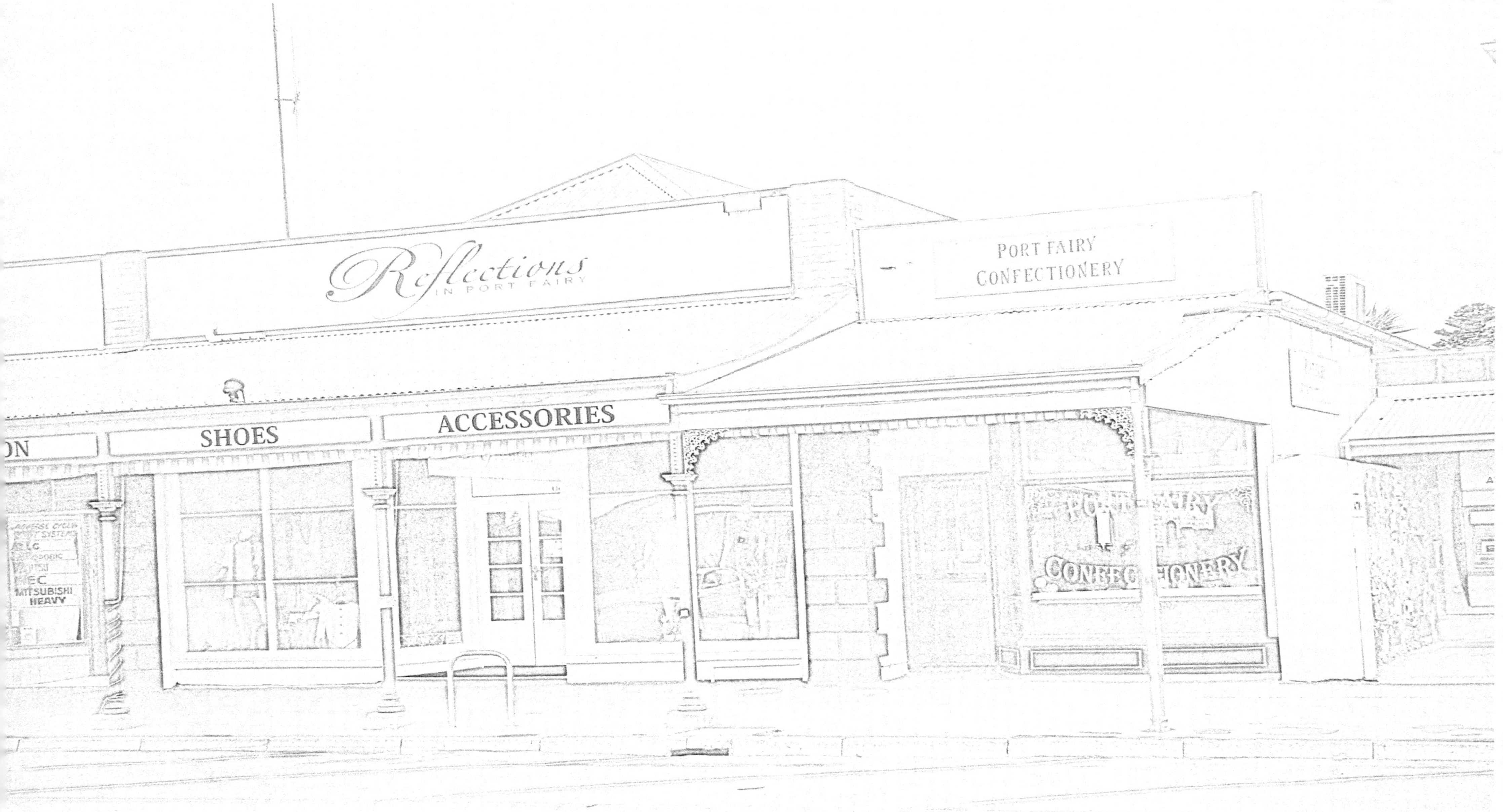
Reflections
IN PORT FAIRY
PORT FAIRY
CONFECTIONERY
ON
SHOES
ACCESSORIES
MITSUBISHI
HEAVY

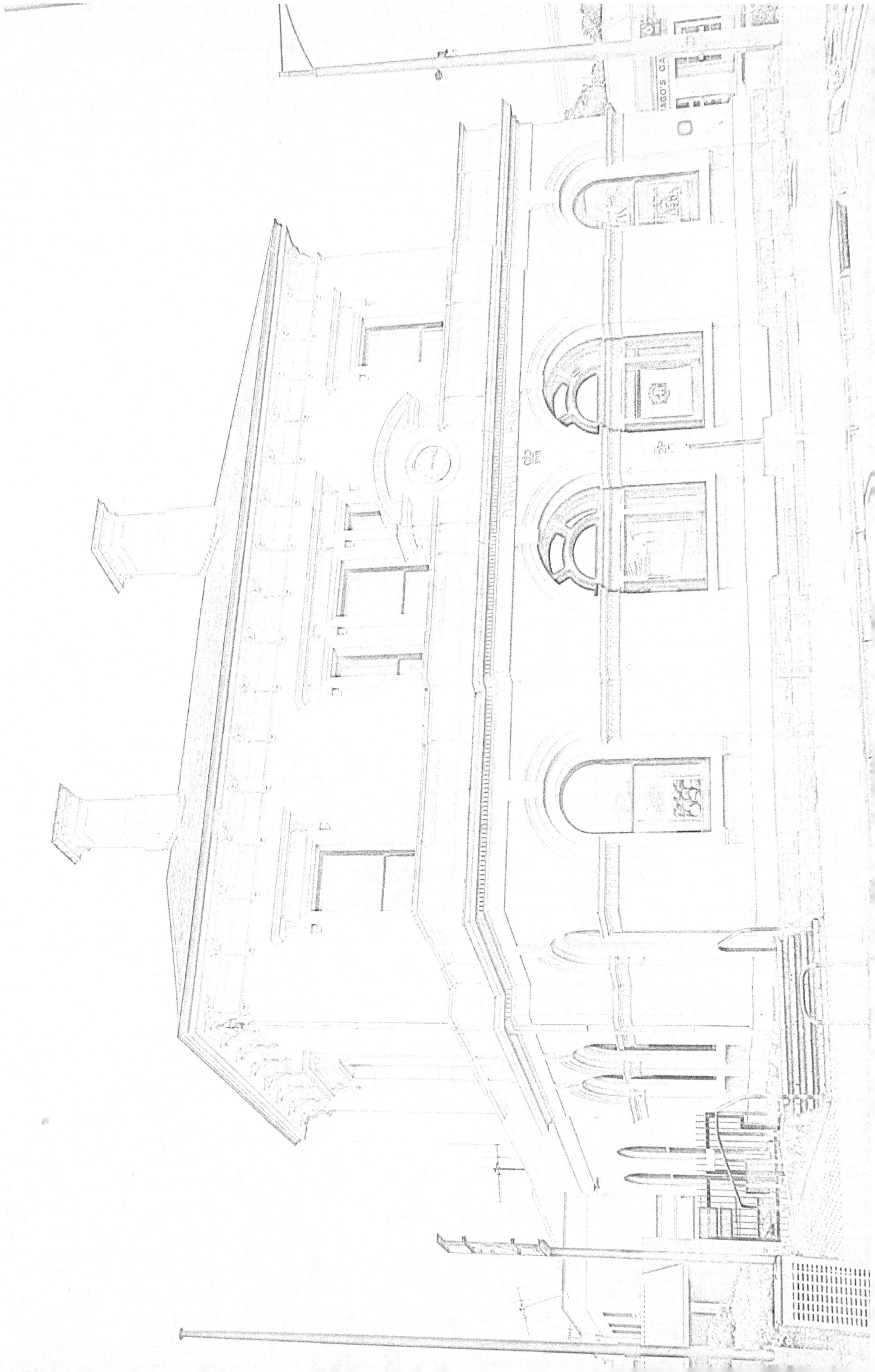

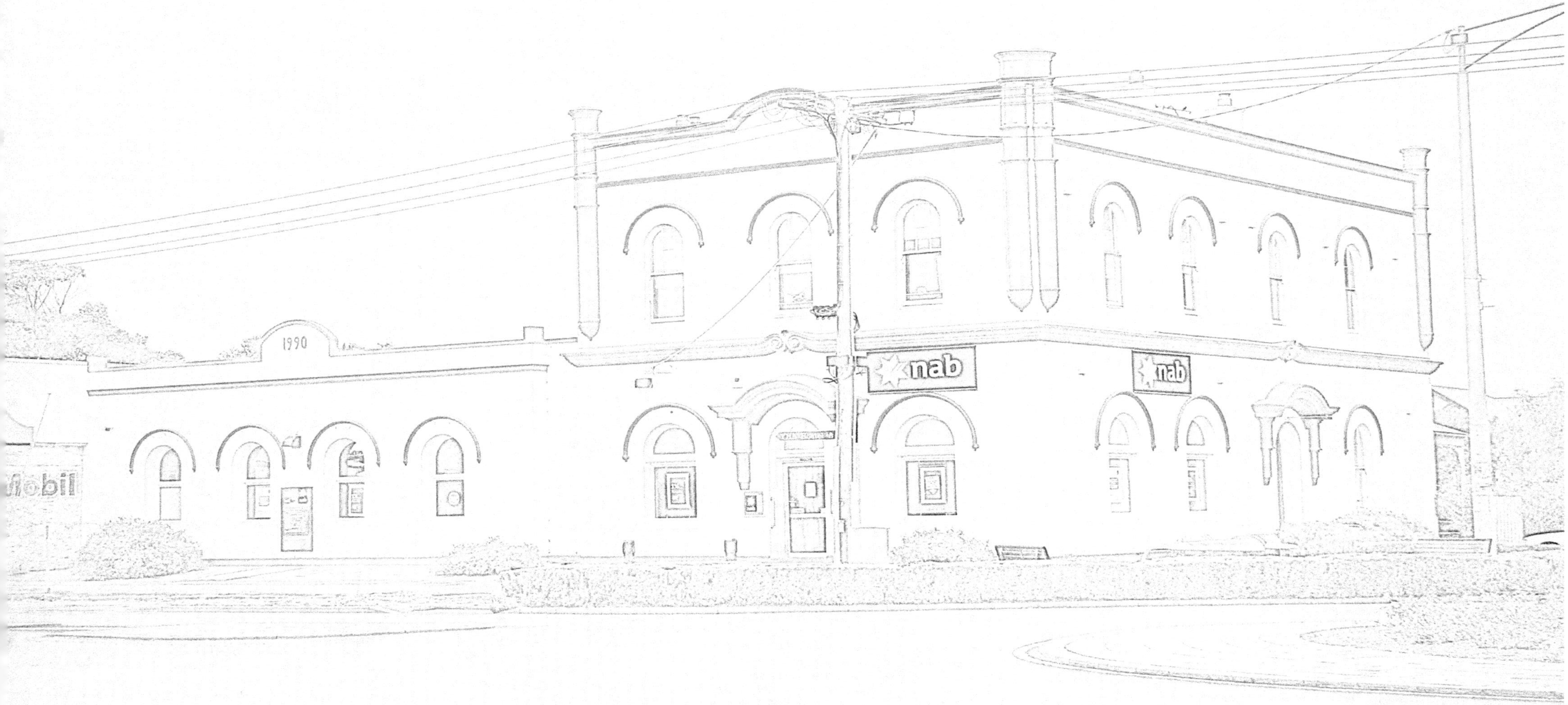
1990
nab
nab
Mobil

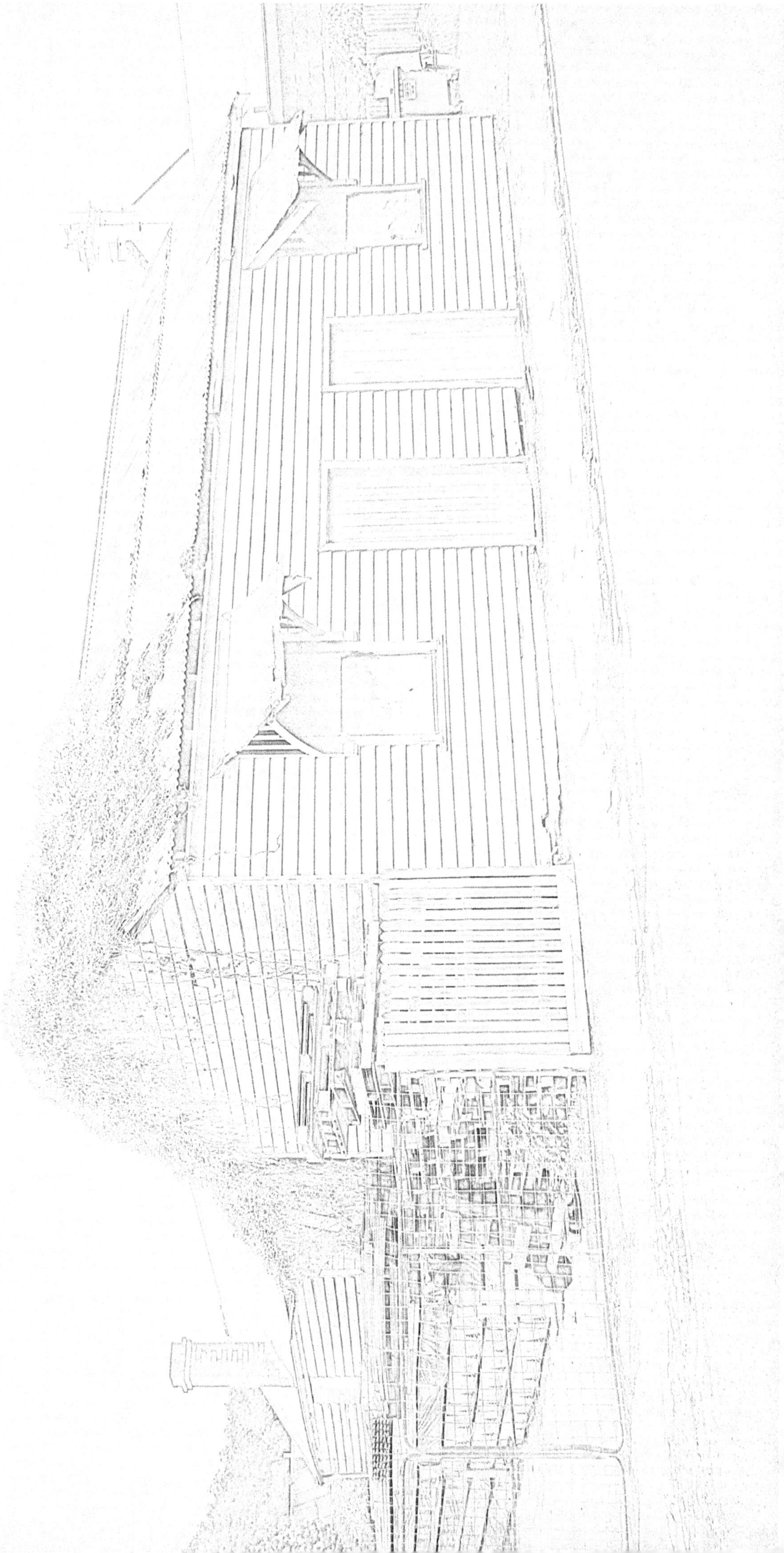

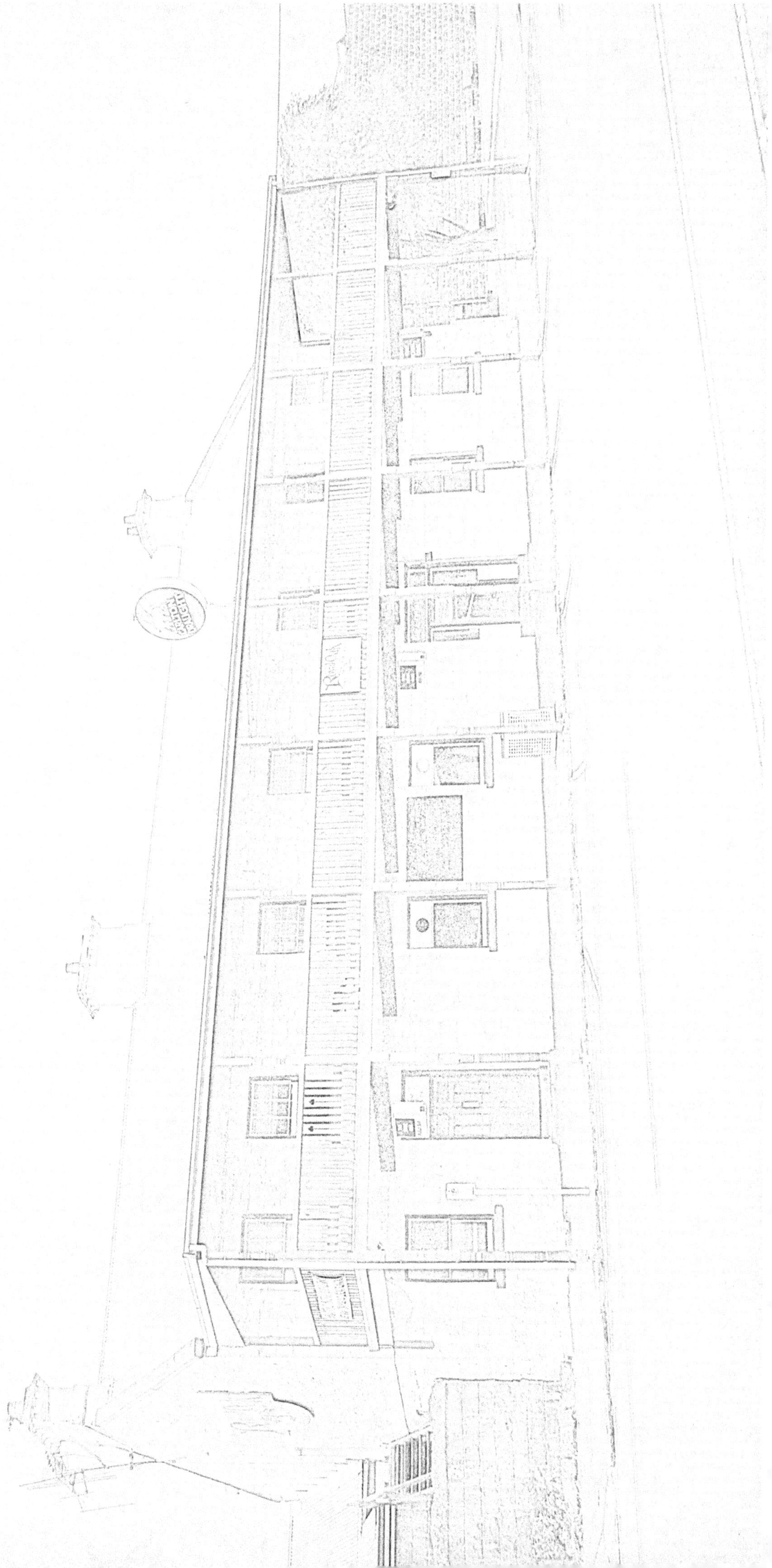

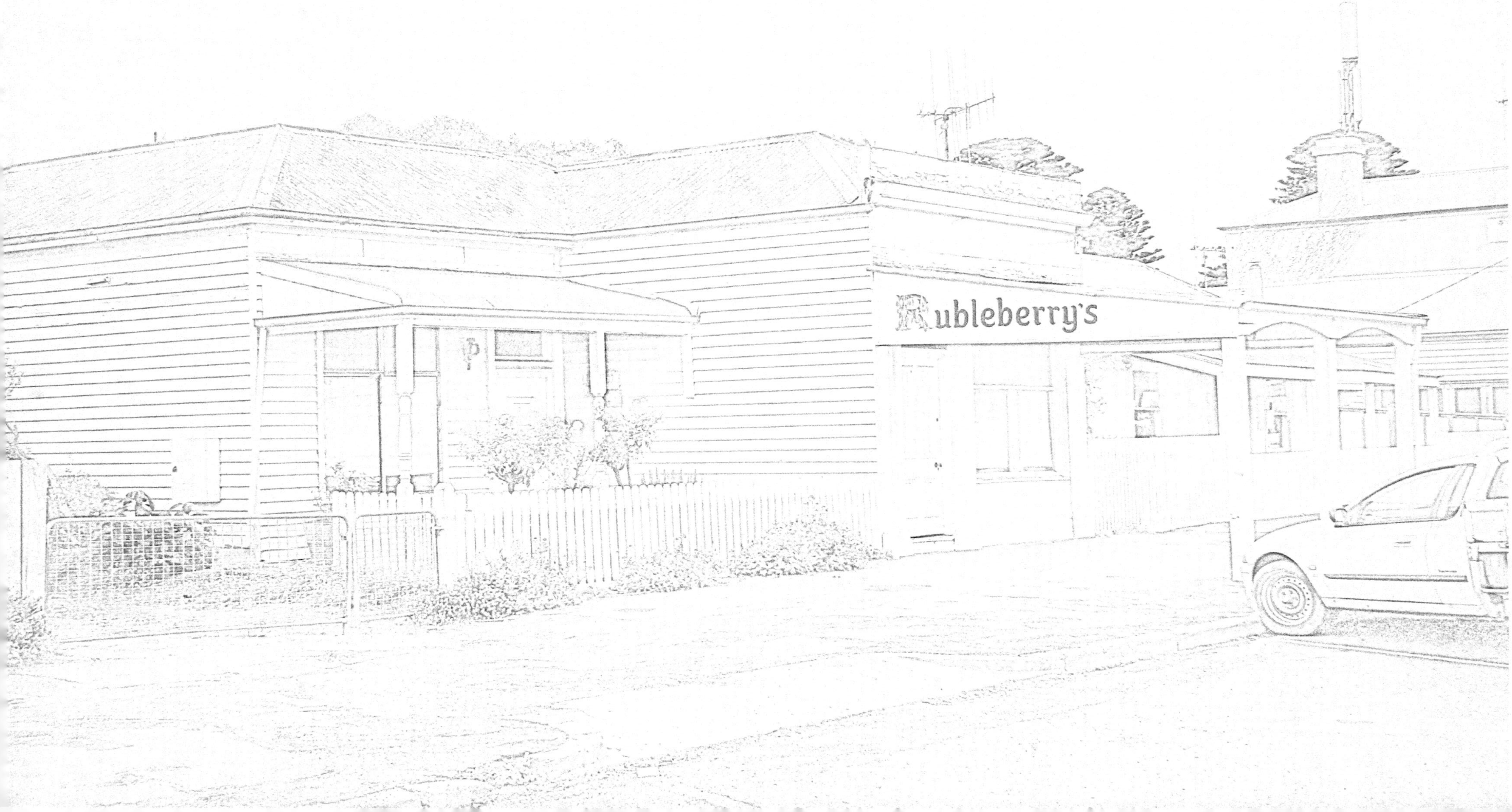
Rubleberry's

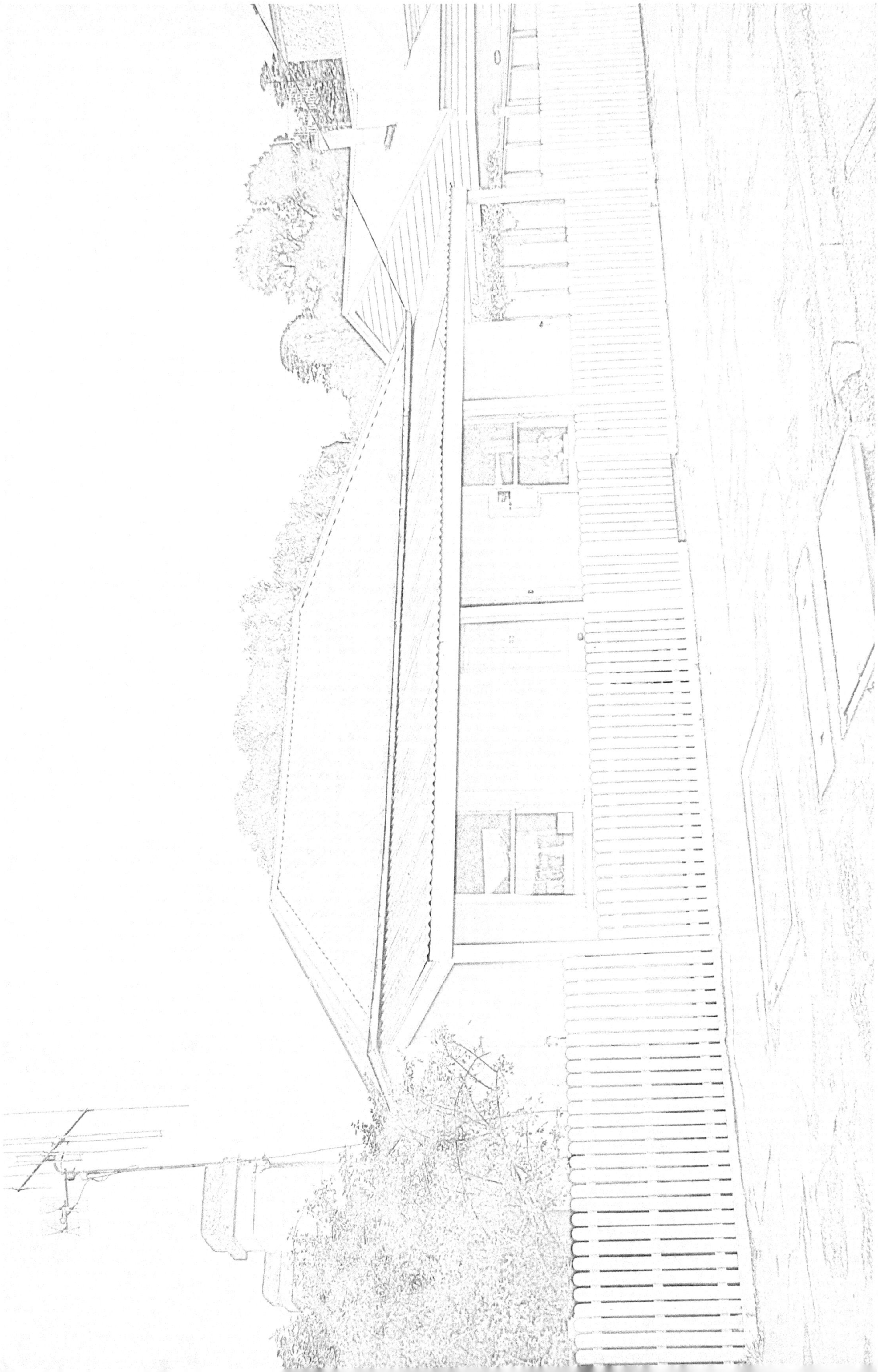

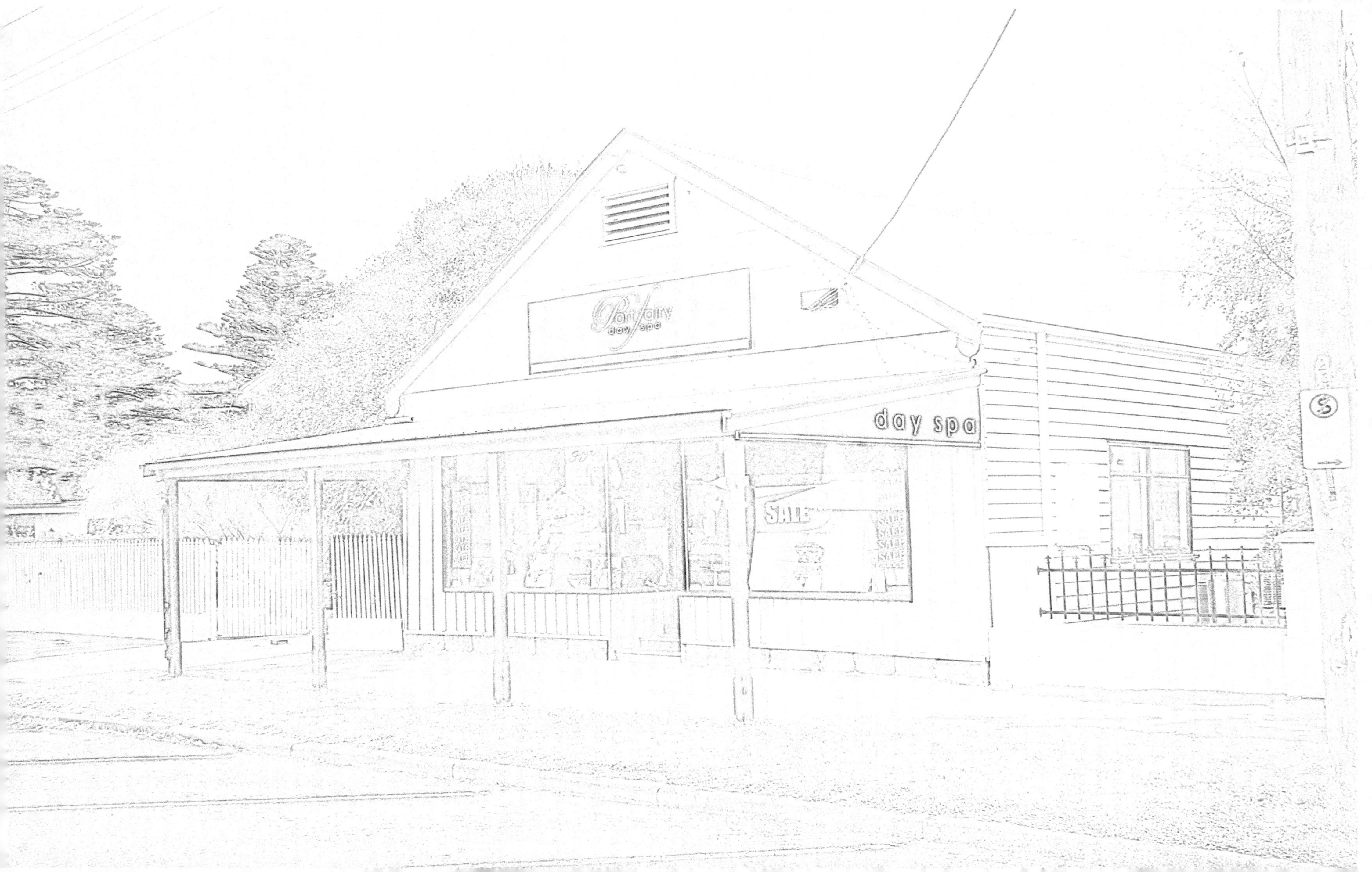

Port Fairy
day spa
day spa
SALE

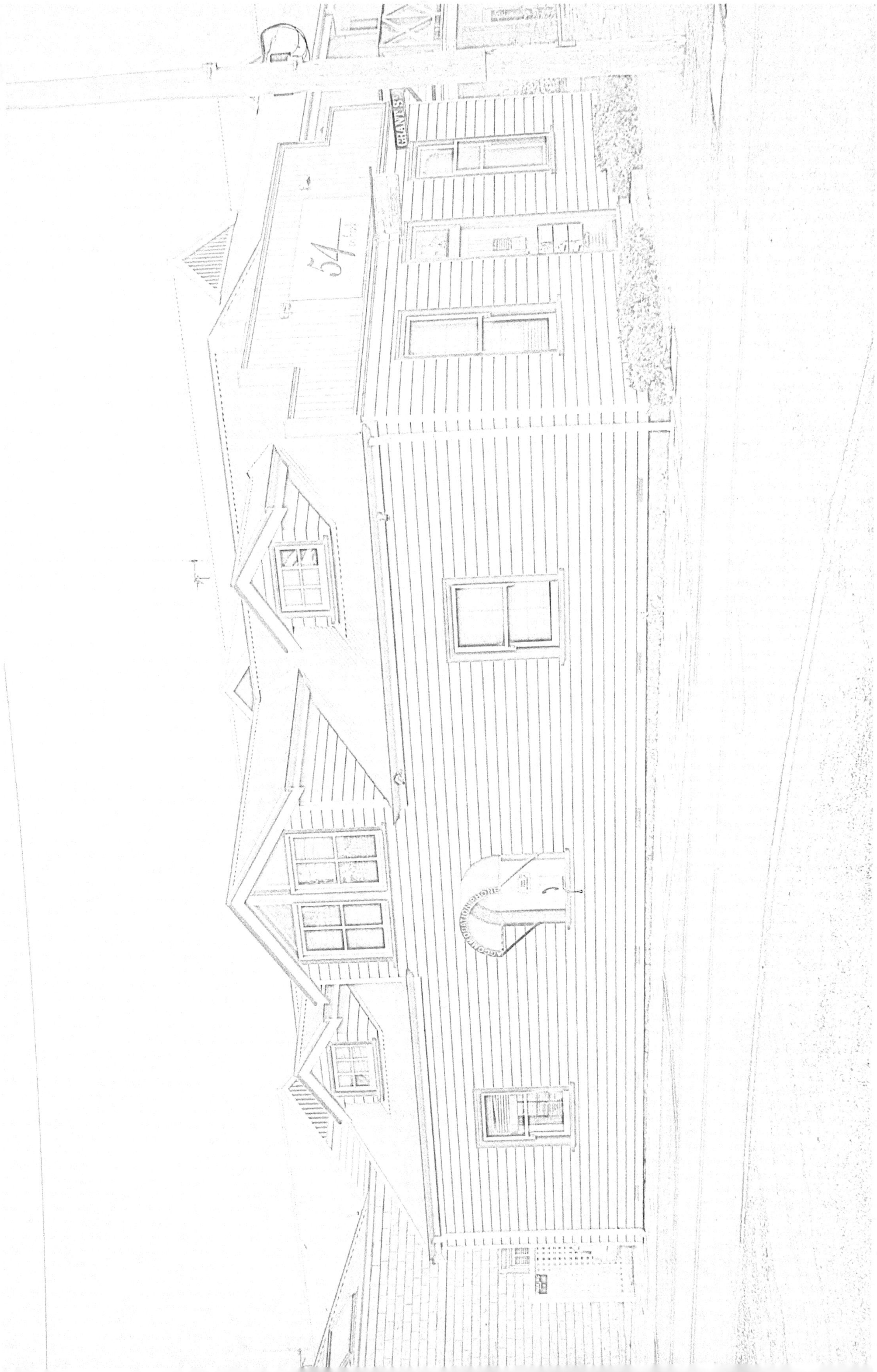
ACCOMMODATION PHONE

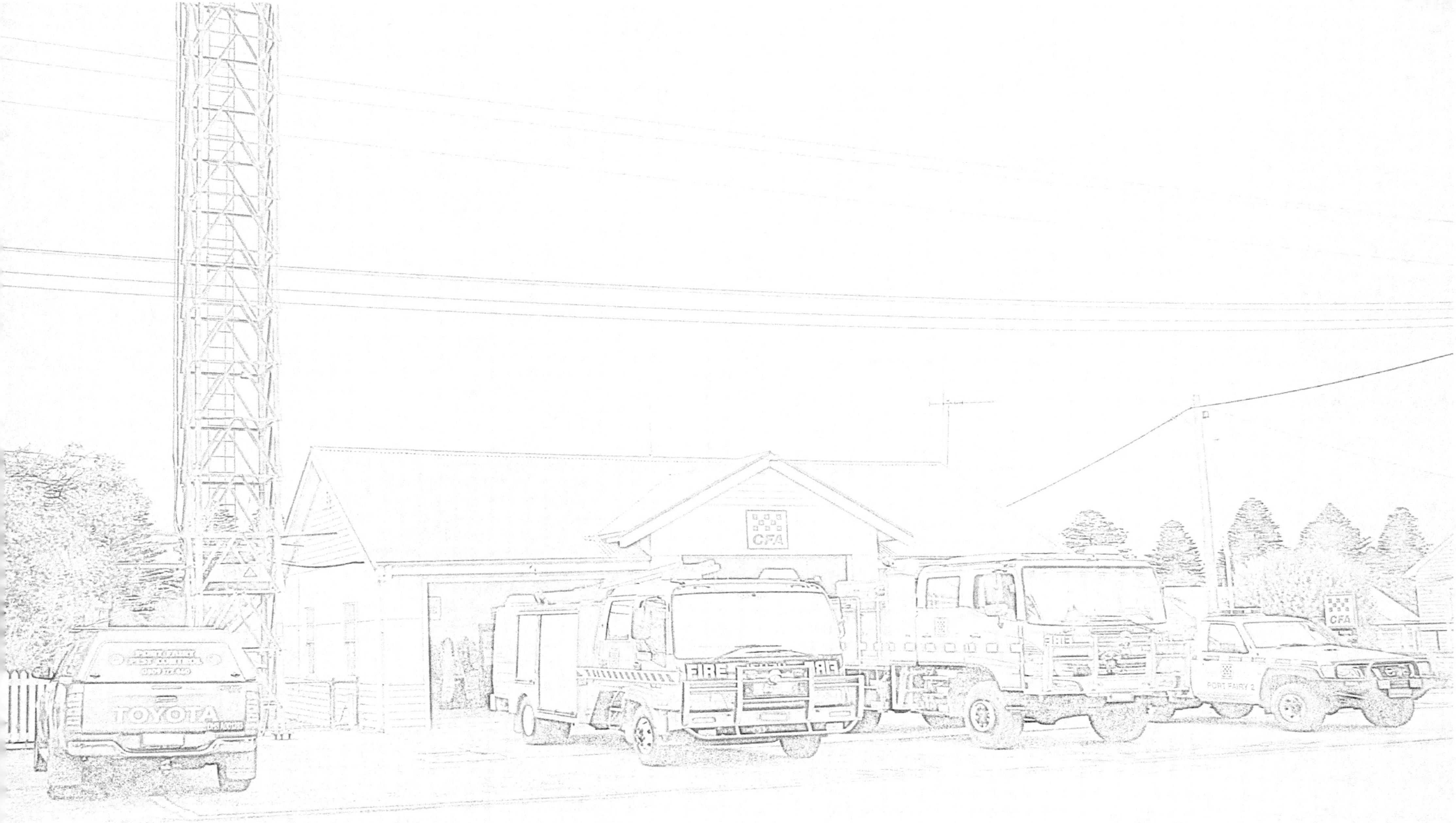

CFA
TOYOTA
FIRE
CFA
PORT FAIRY 2

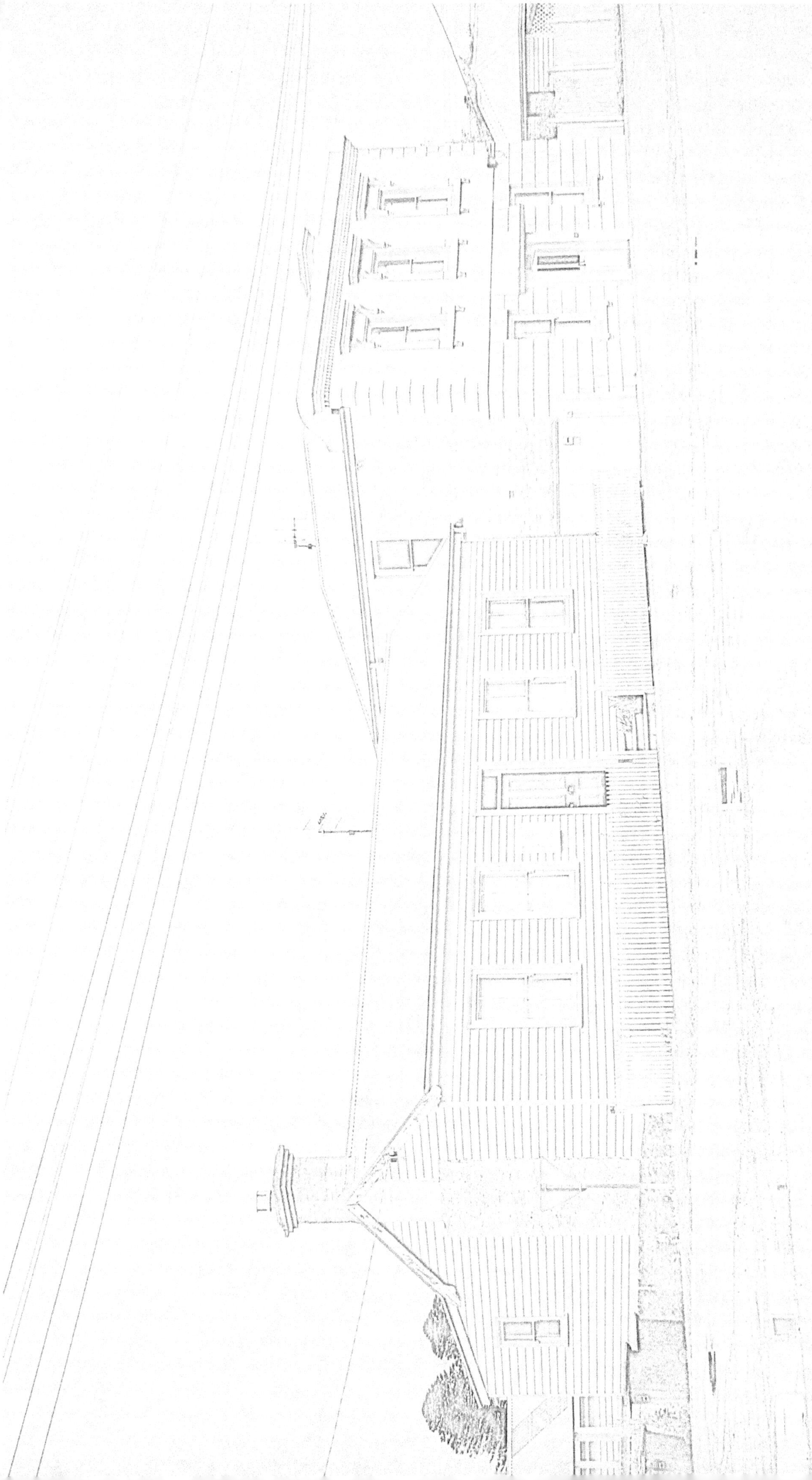

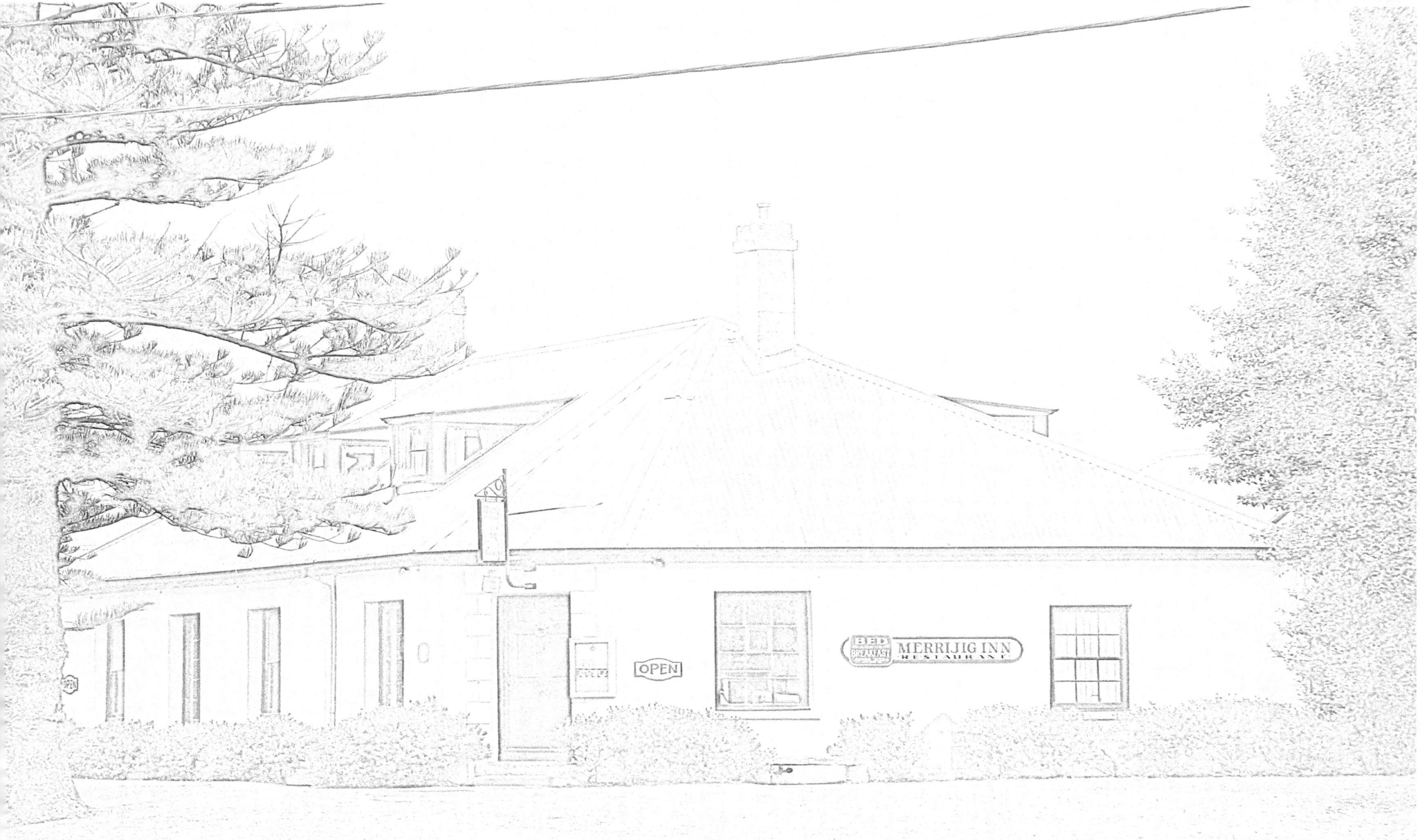
BED BREAKFAST
MERRIJIG INN
RESTAURANT
OPEN

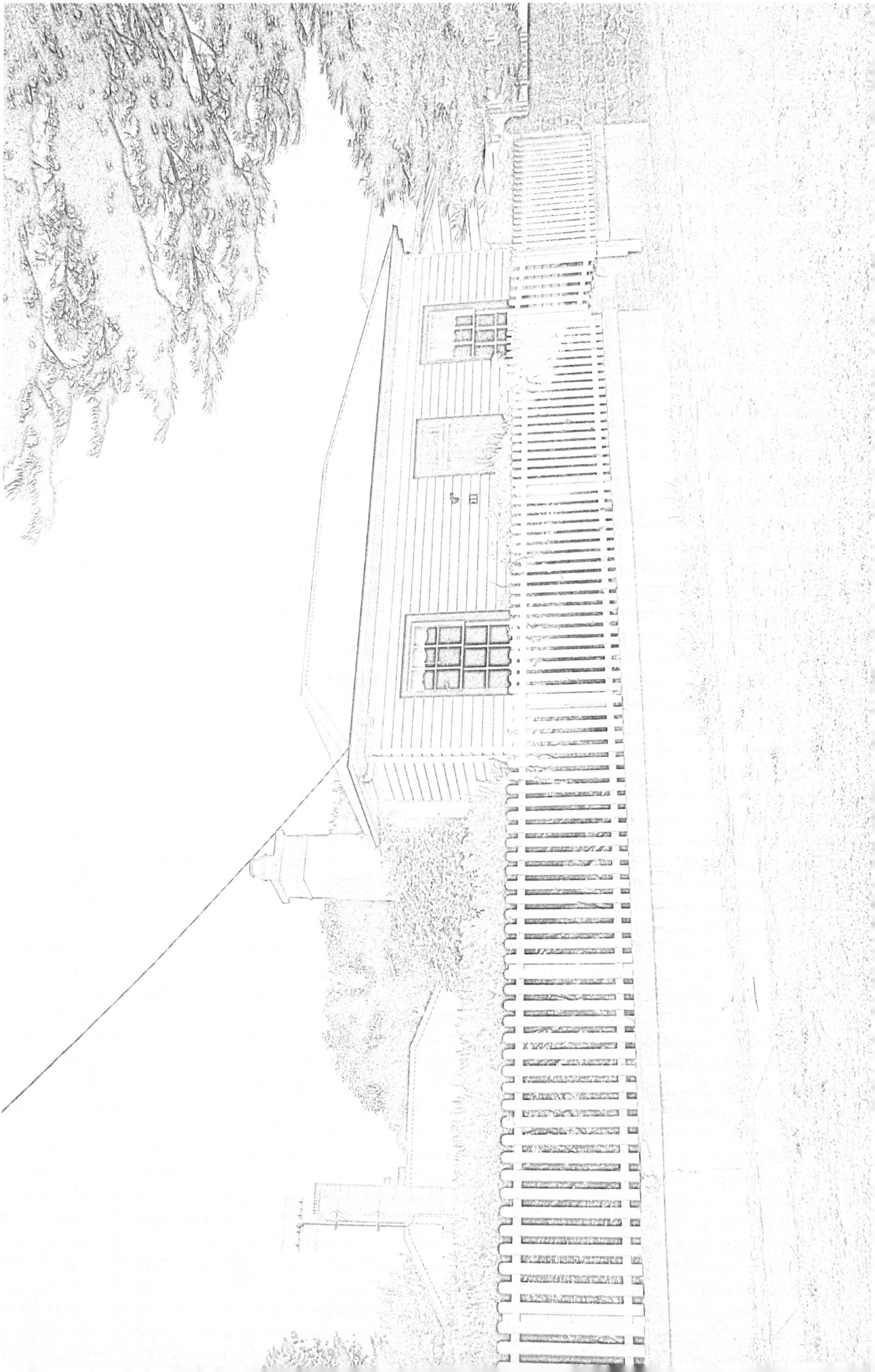

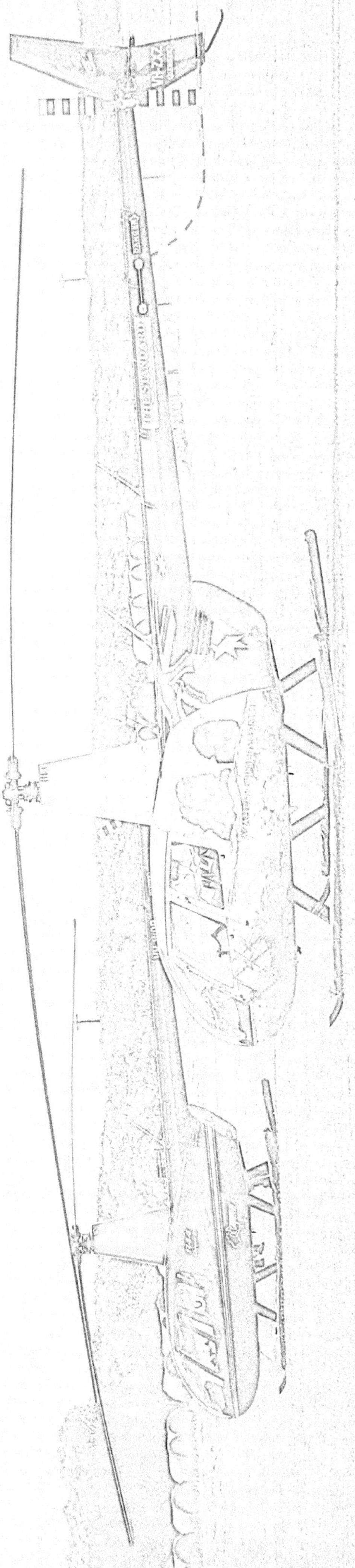

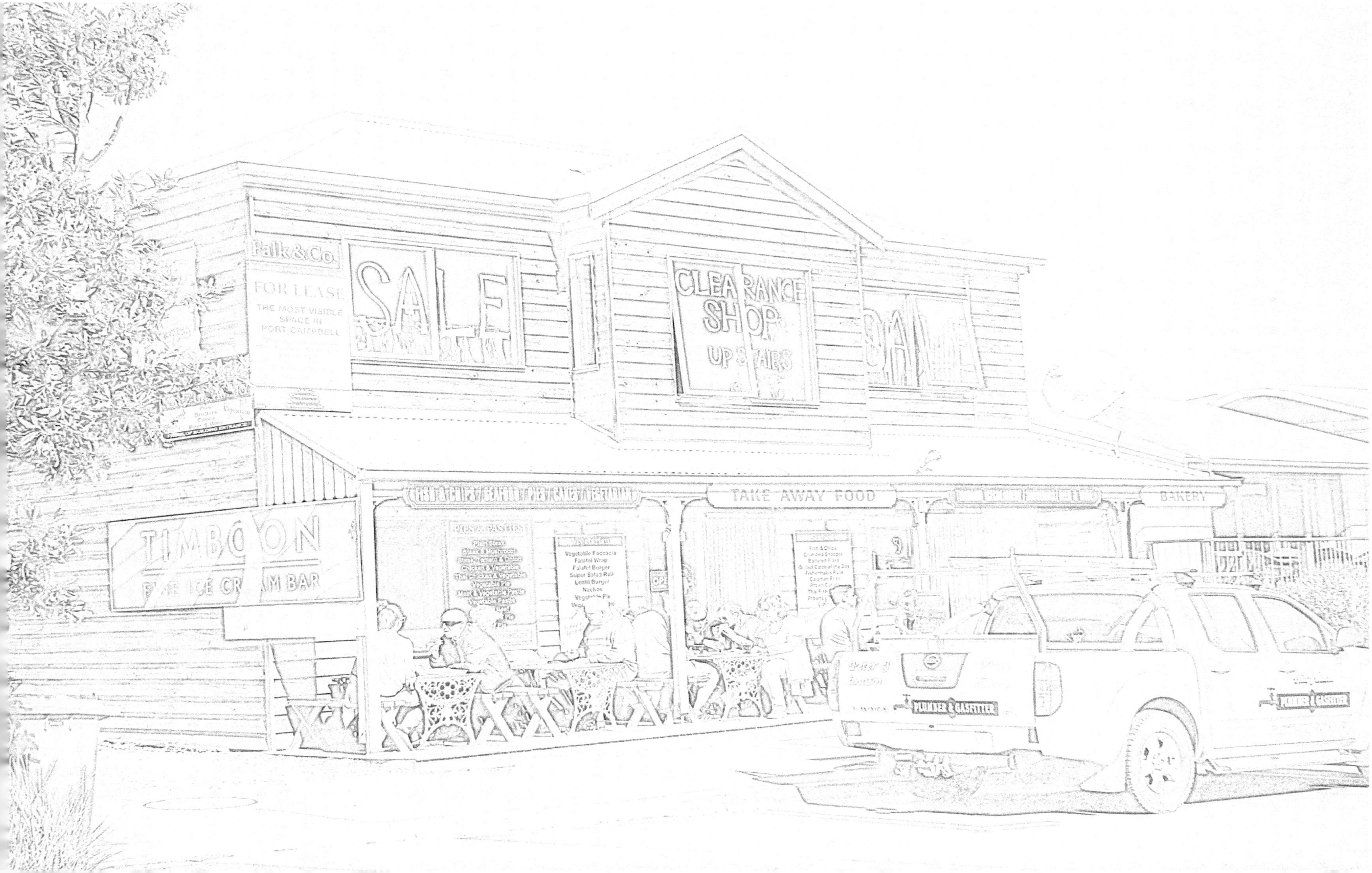
Falk&Co.
FOR LEASE
THE MOST VISIBLE
SPACE IN
PORT CAMPBELL
SALE
CLEARANCE
SHOP
UP STAIRS
TIMBOON
TAKE AWAY FOOD
BAKERY
PLUMBER & GASFITTER

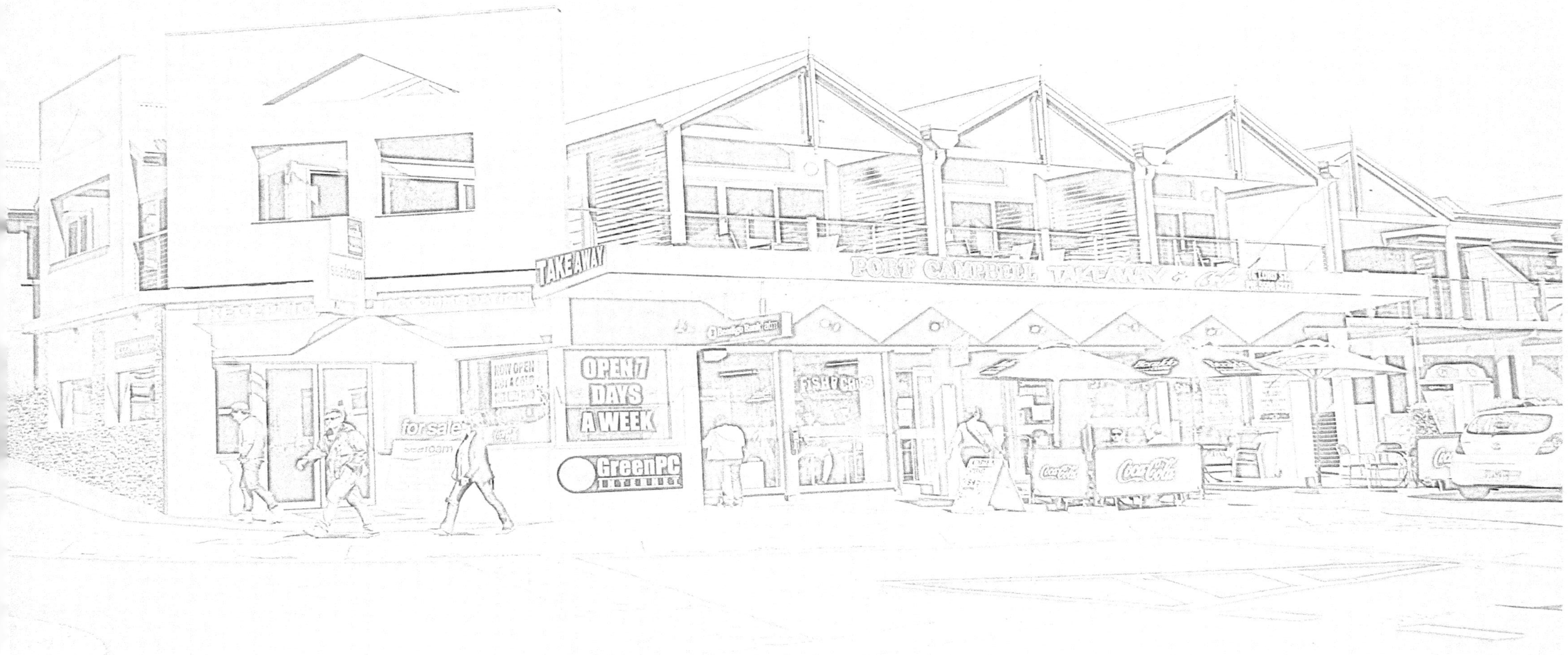
TAKEAWAY
PORT CAMPBELL TAKEAWAY
OPEN 7
DAYS
A WEEK
GreenPC
FISH & CHIPS
for sale
Coca-Cola
Coca-Cola

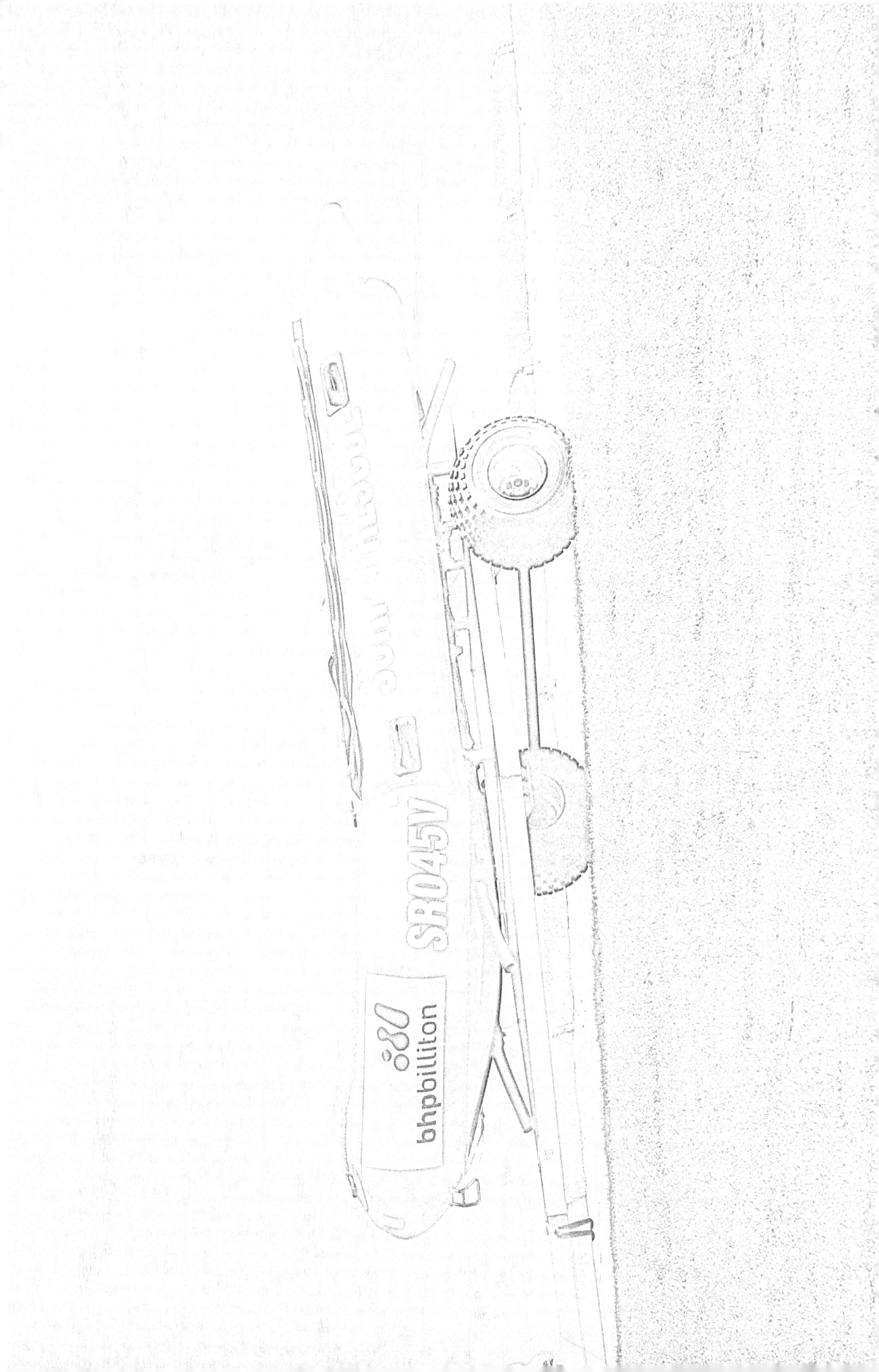
SR045V
bhpbilliton

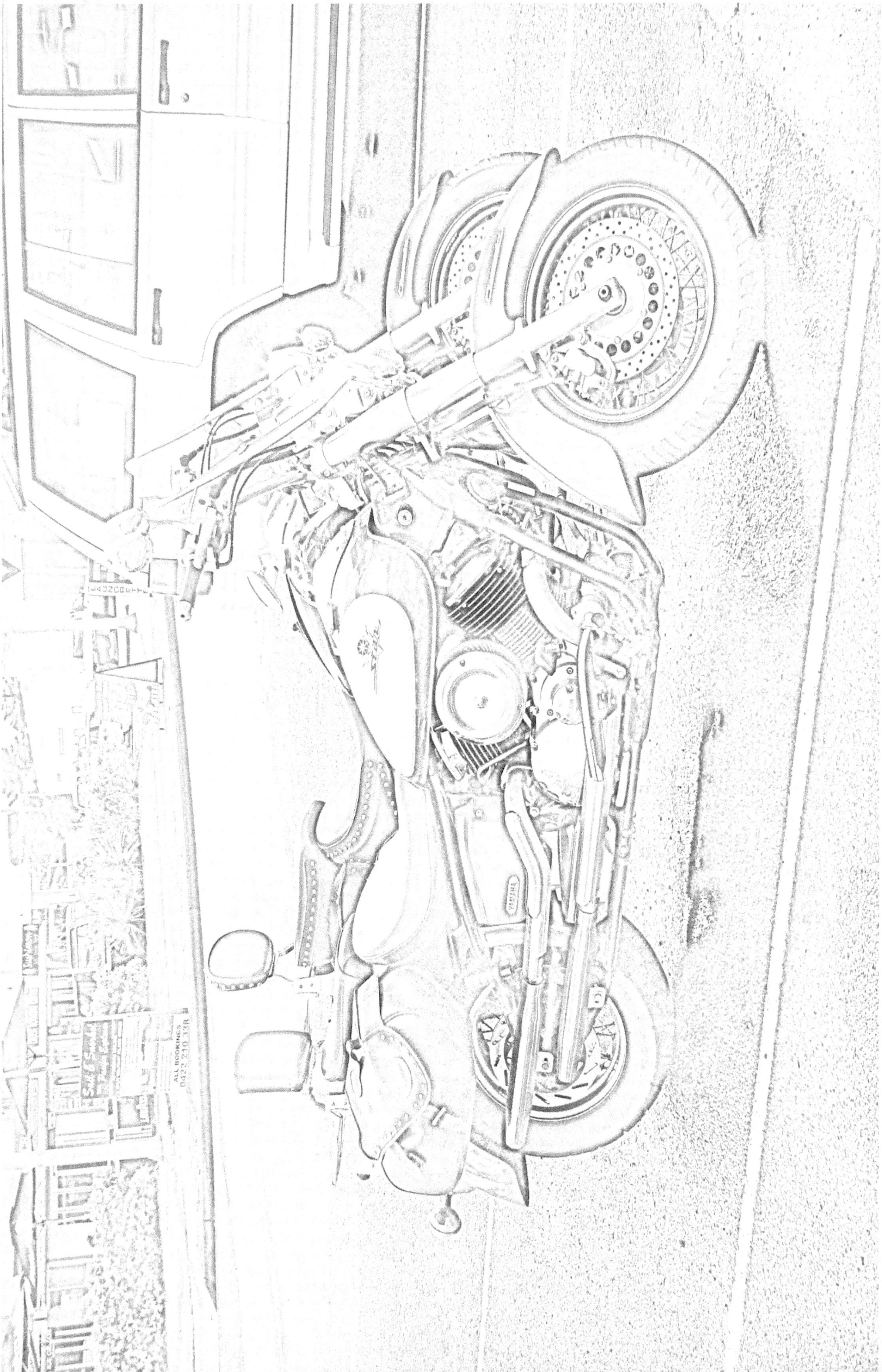

ALL BOOKINGS
YAMAHA

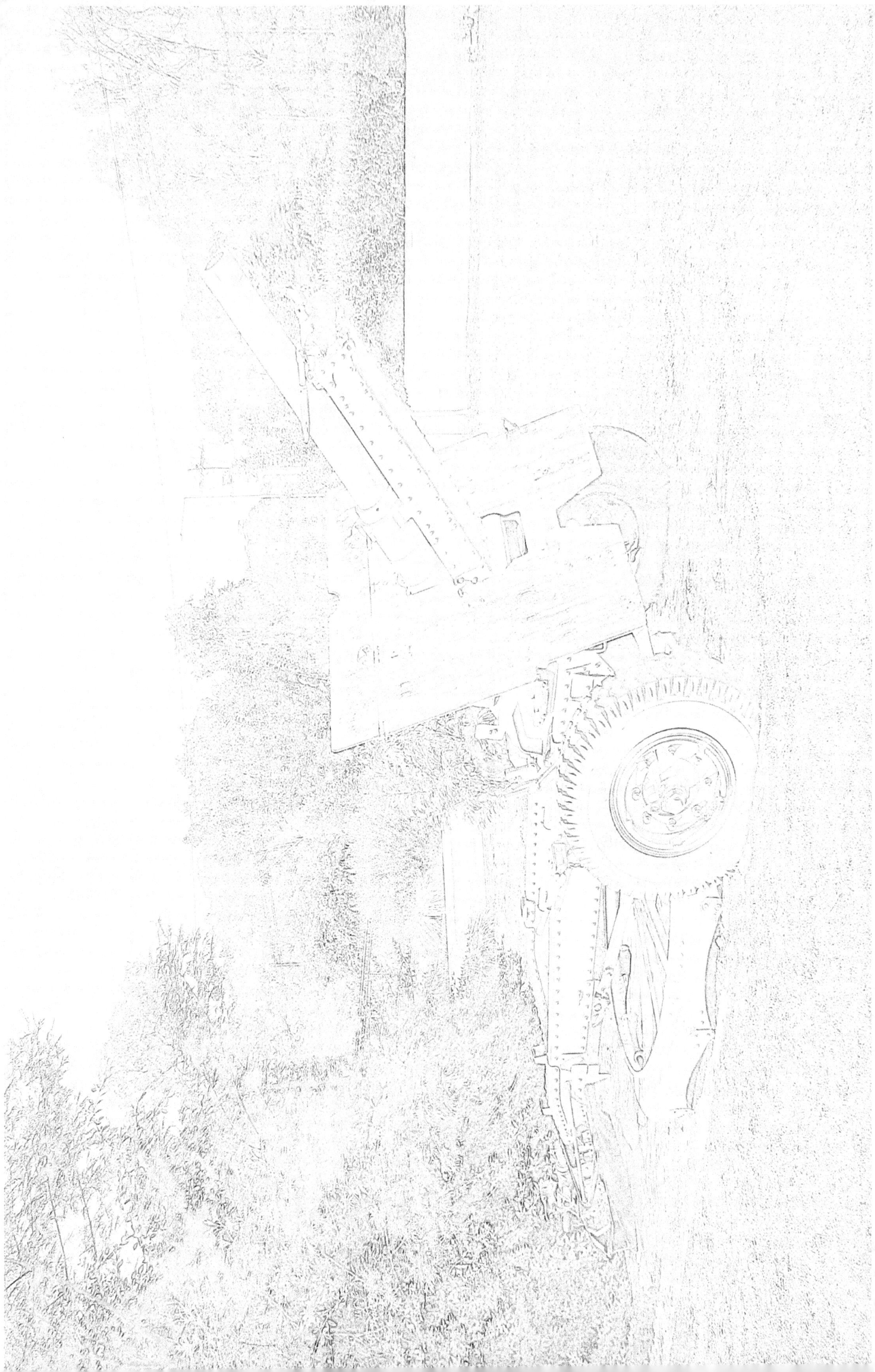

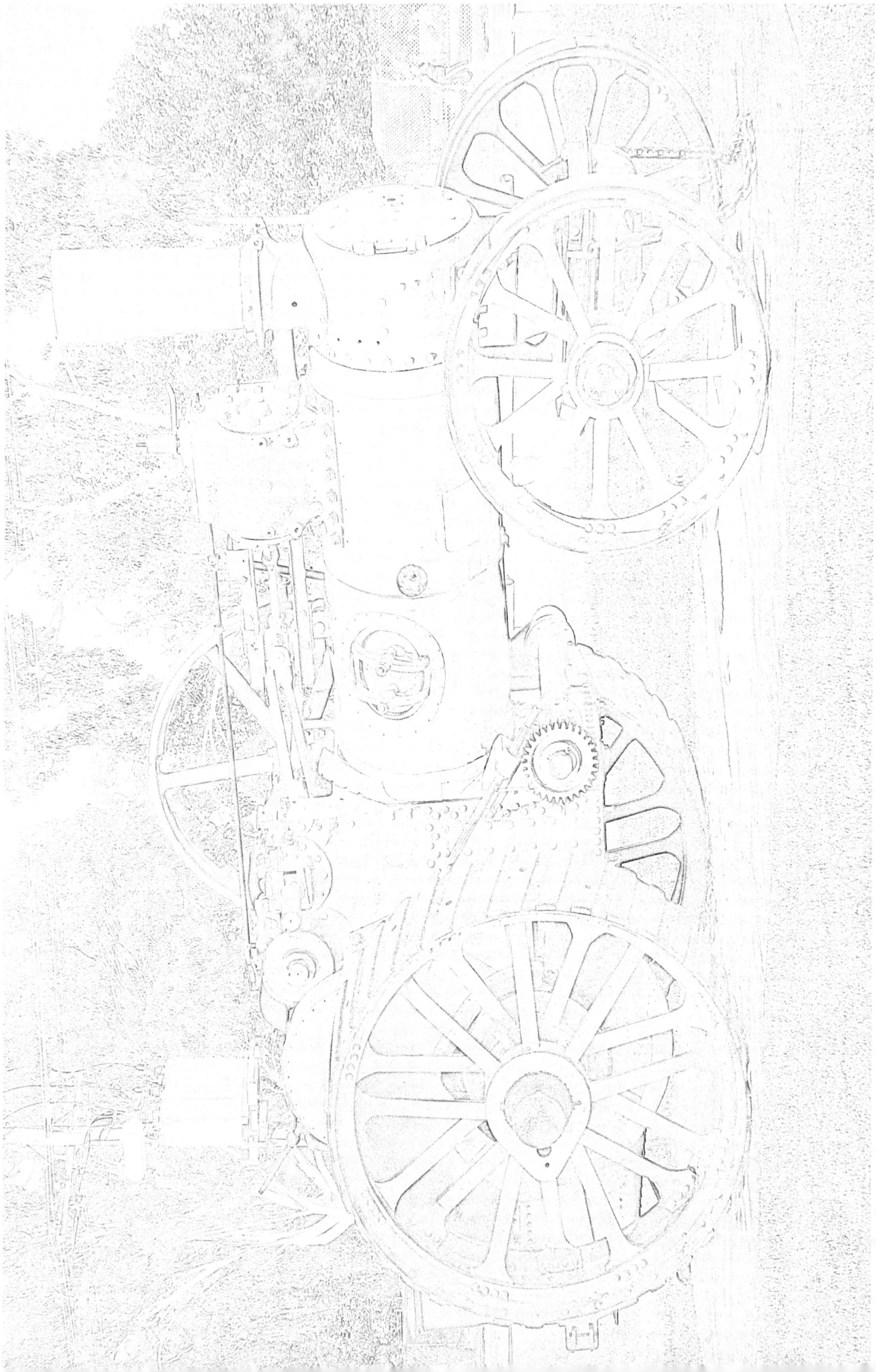

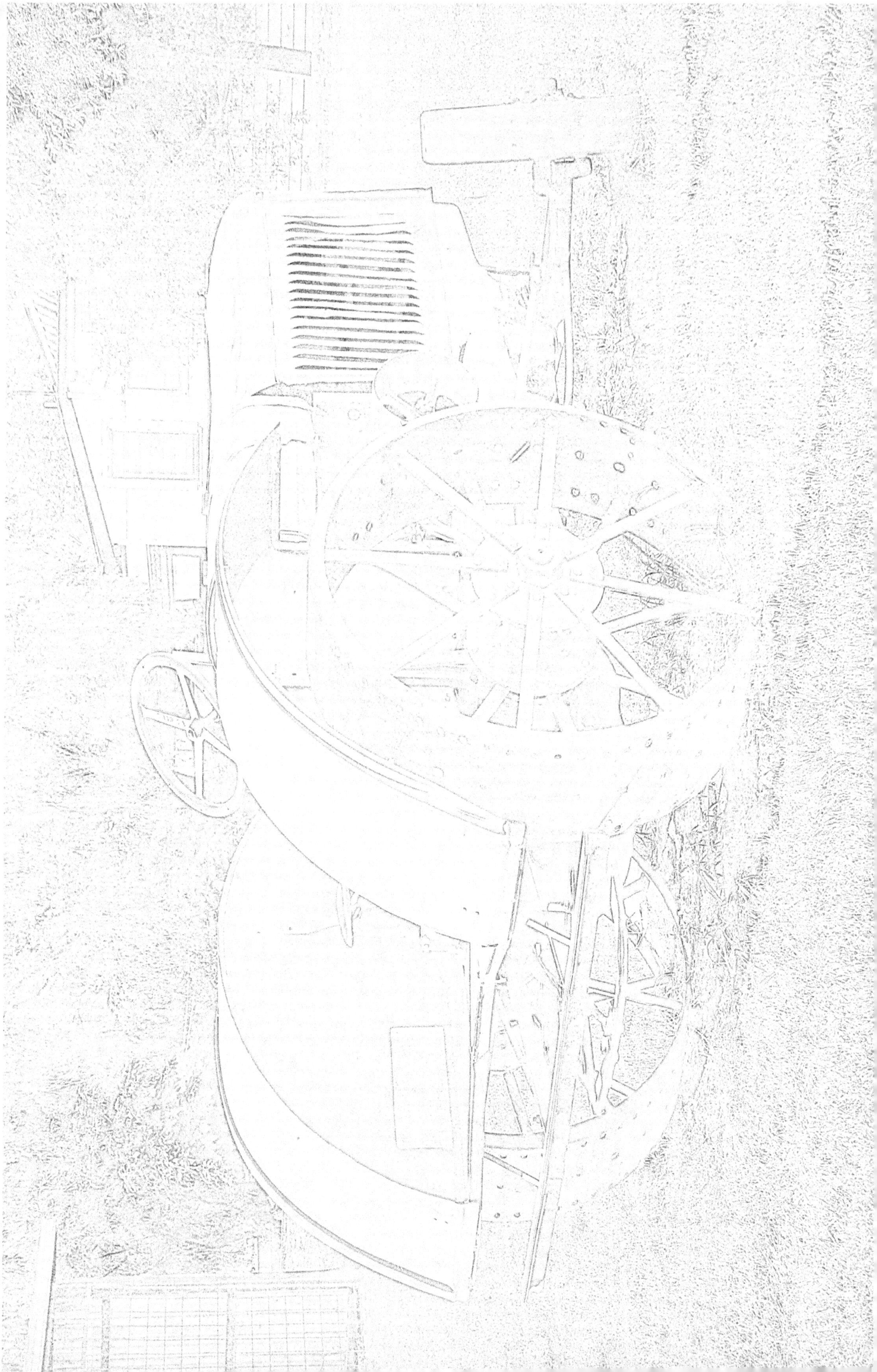

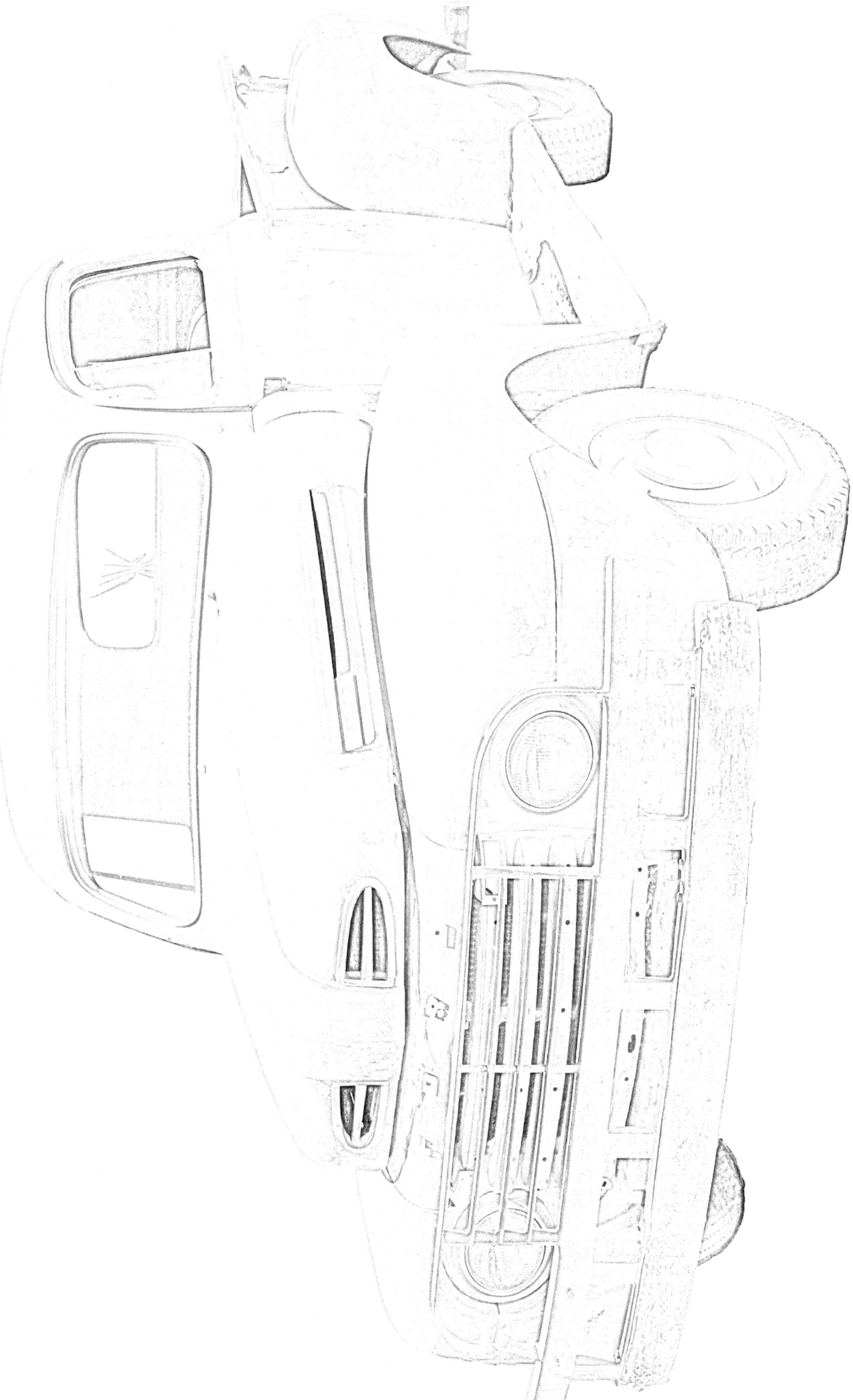

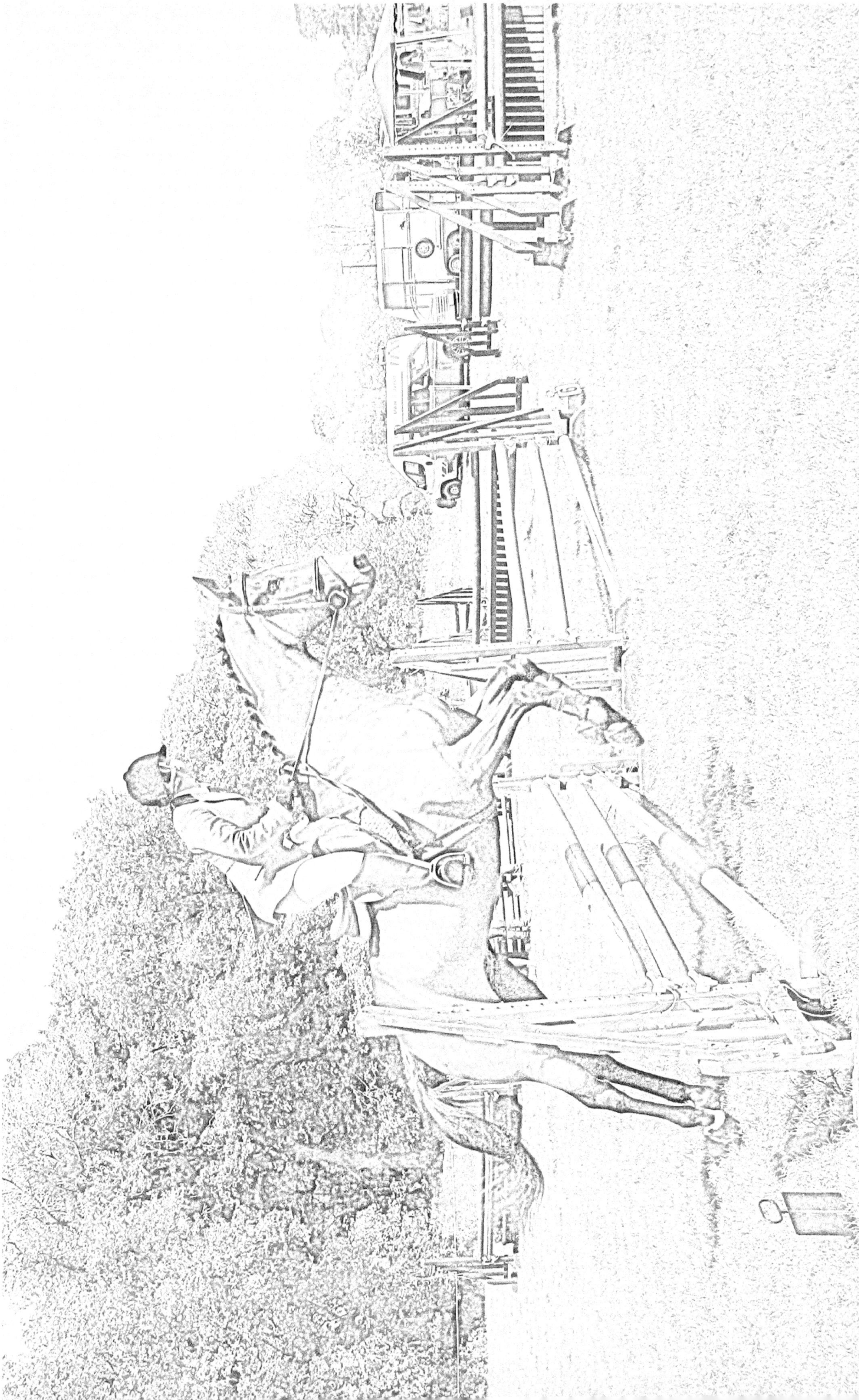

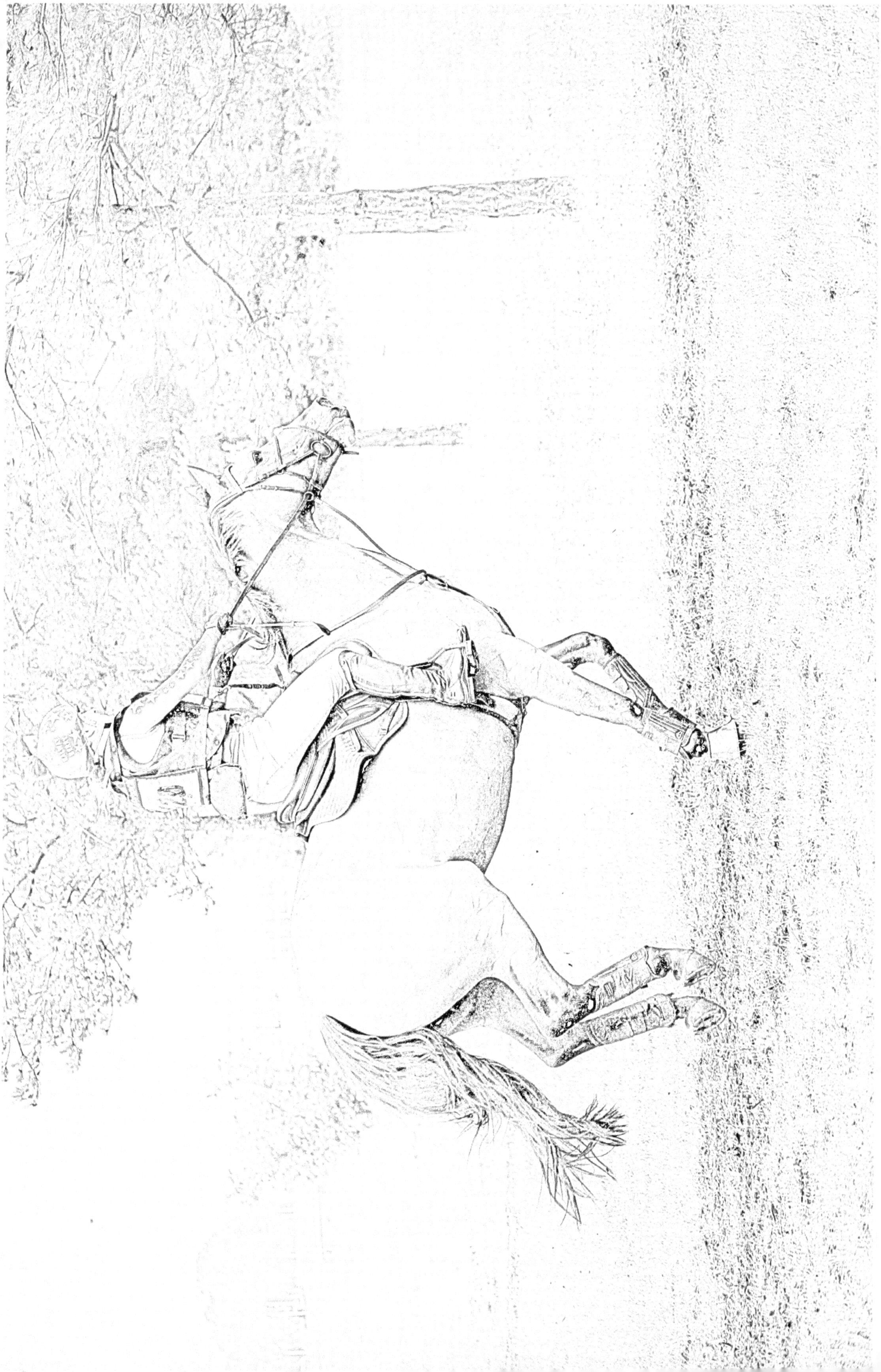

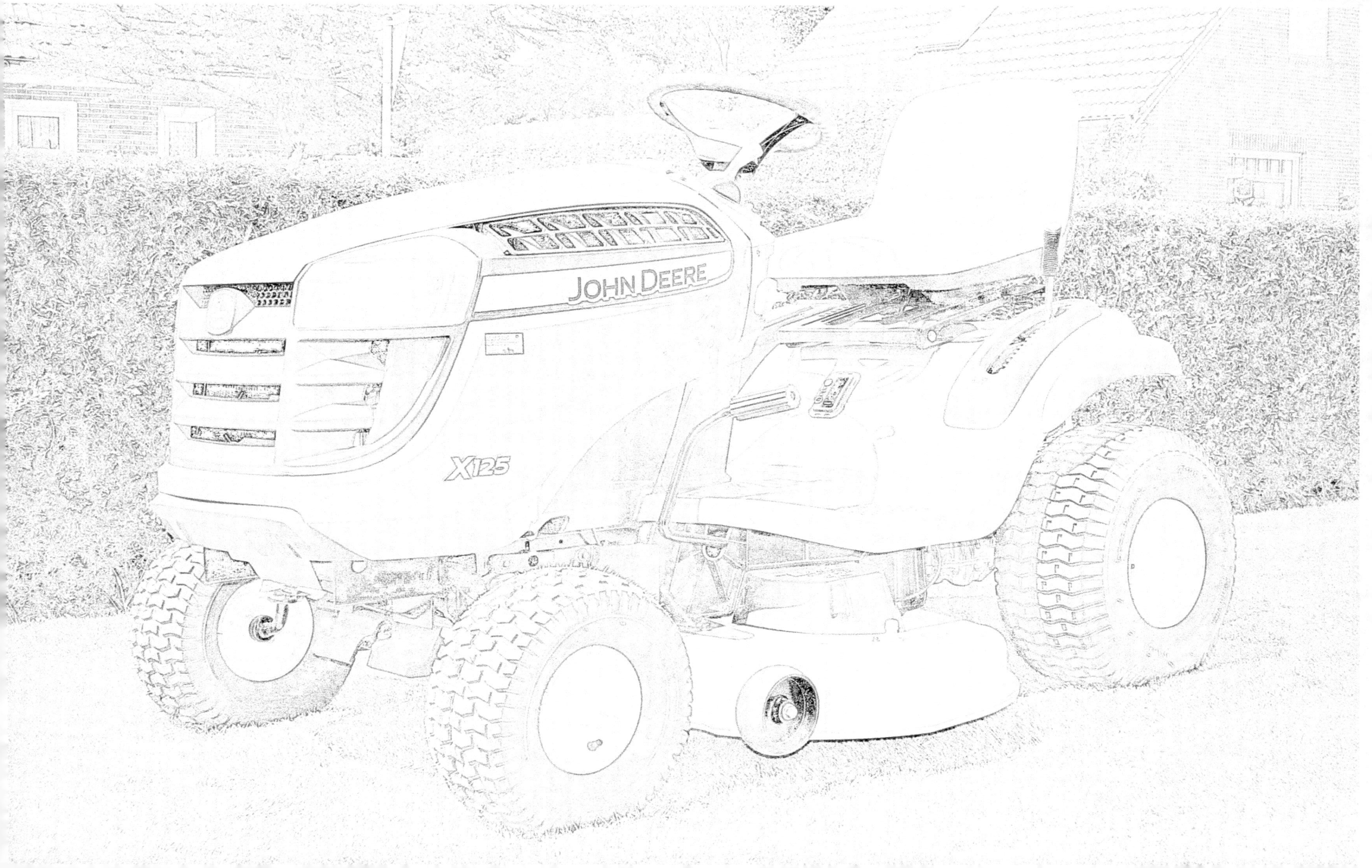
JOHN DEERE
X125

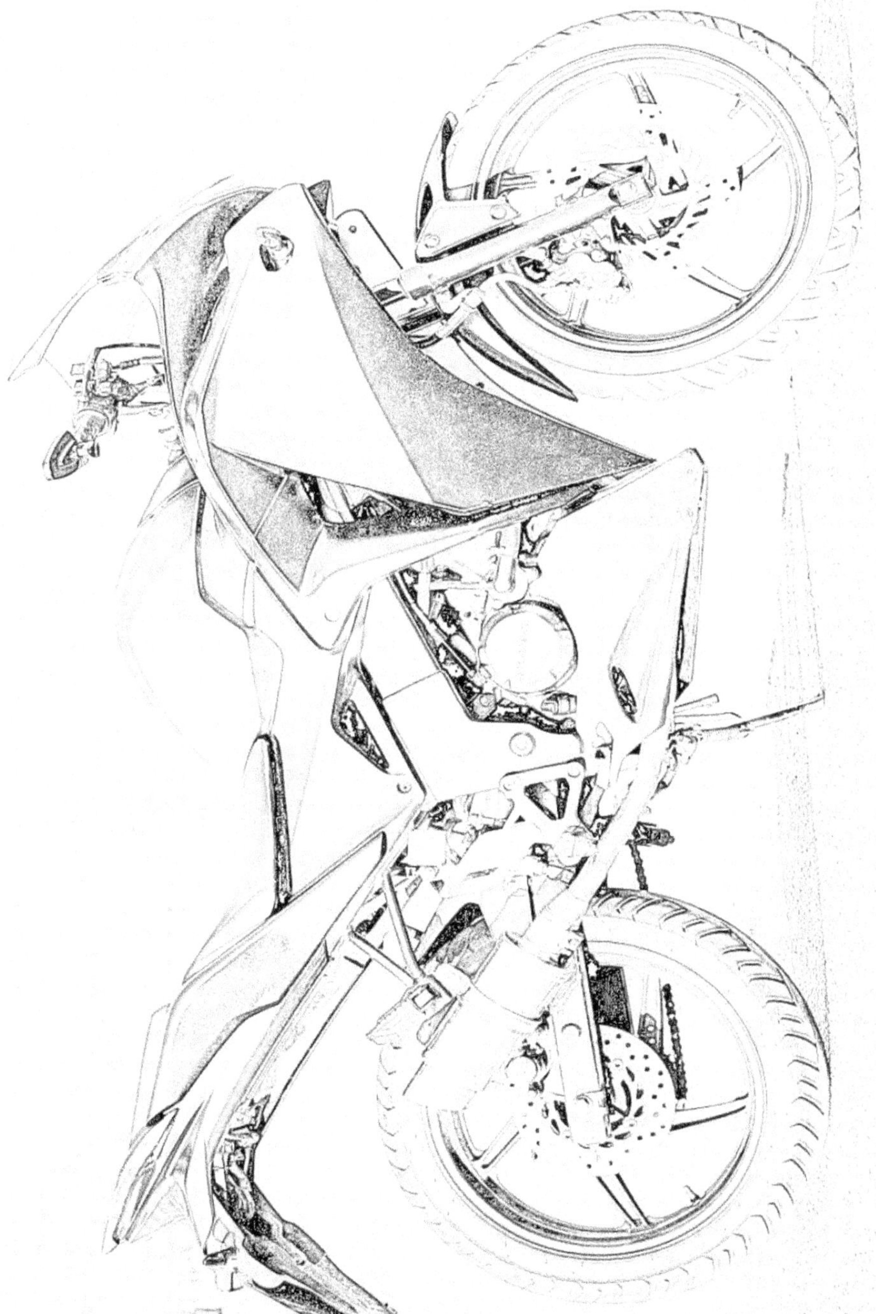

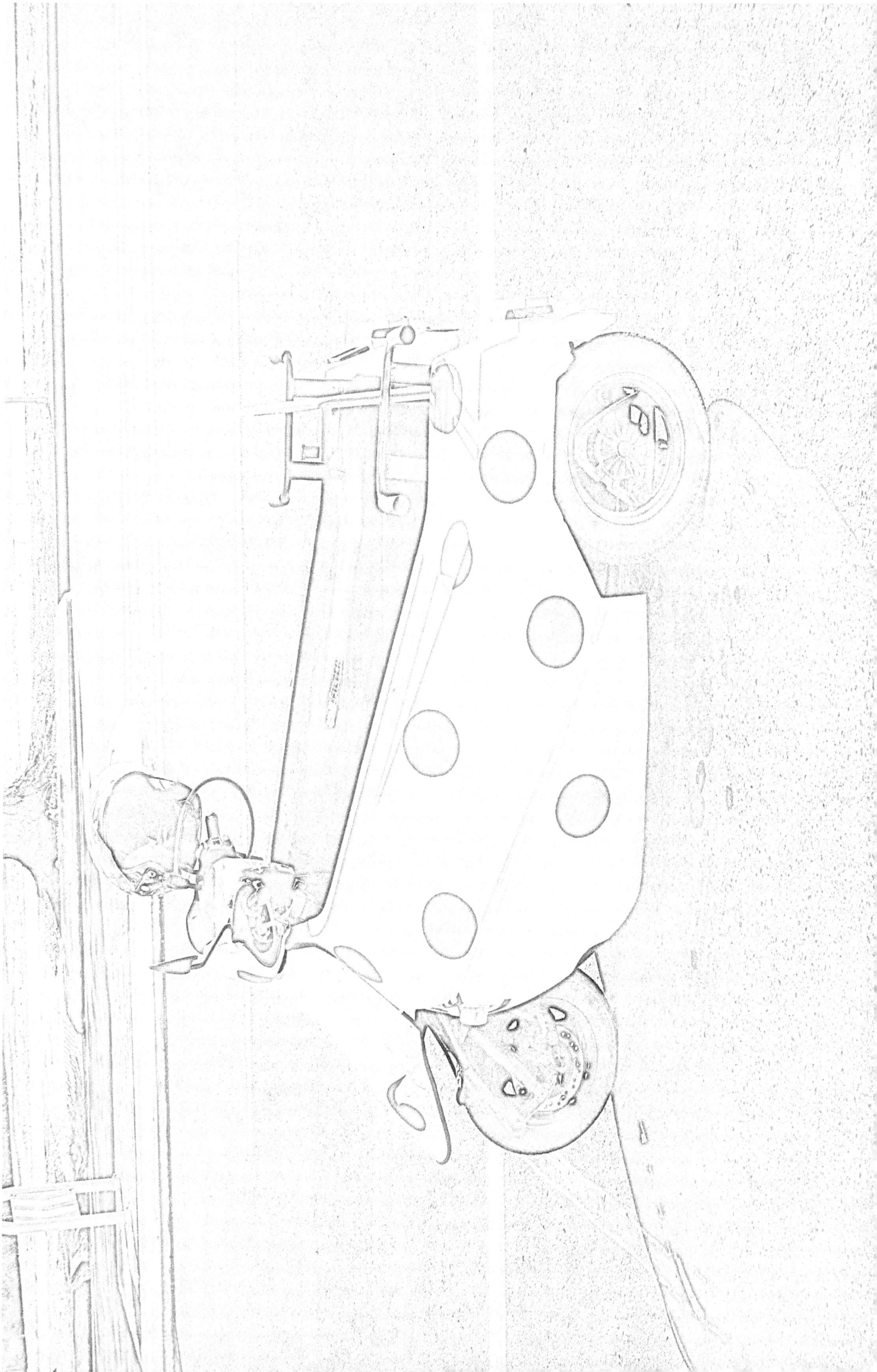

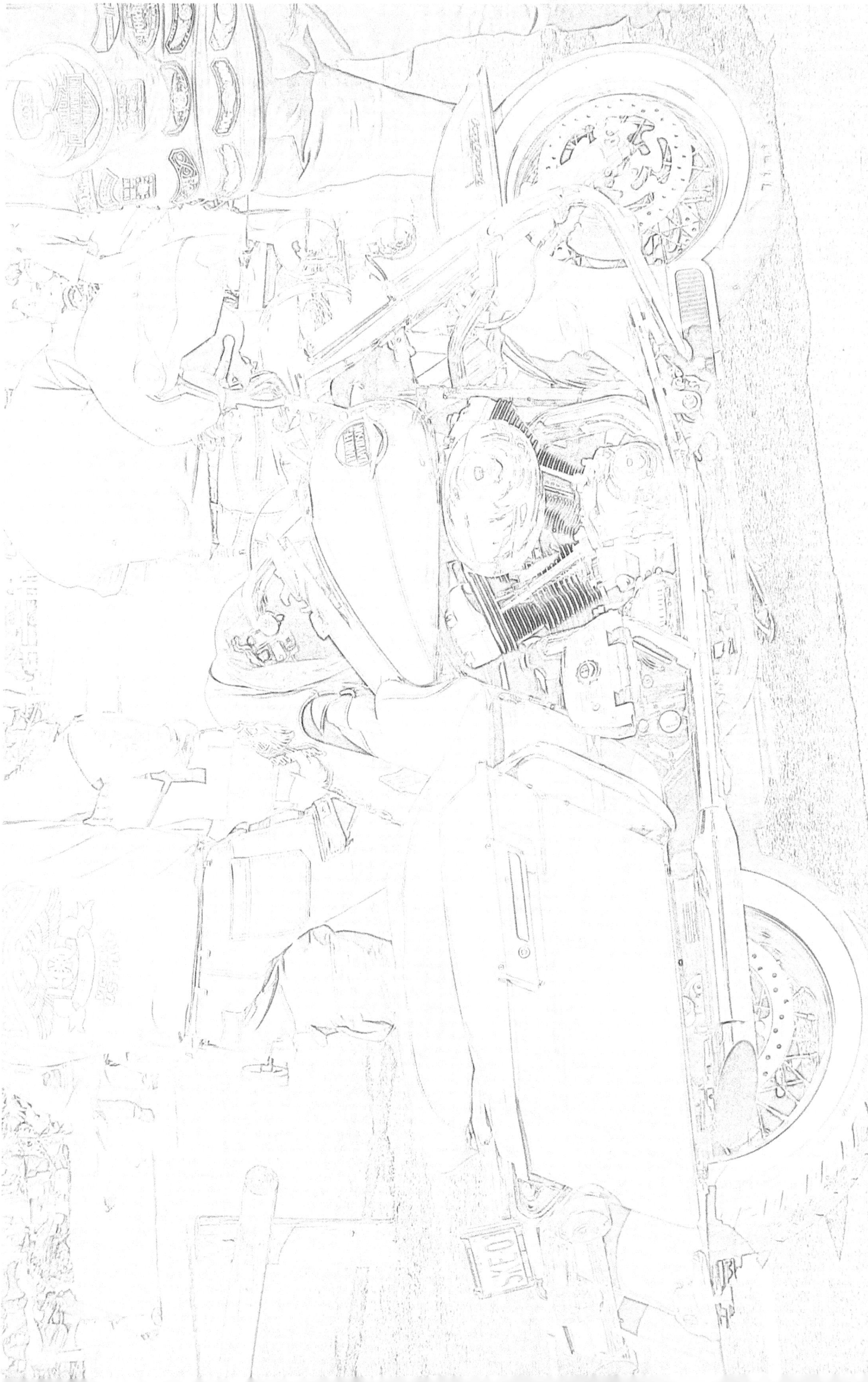

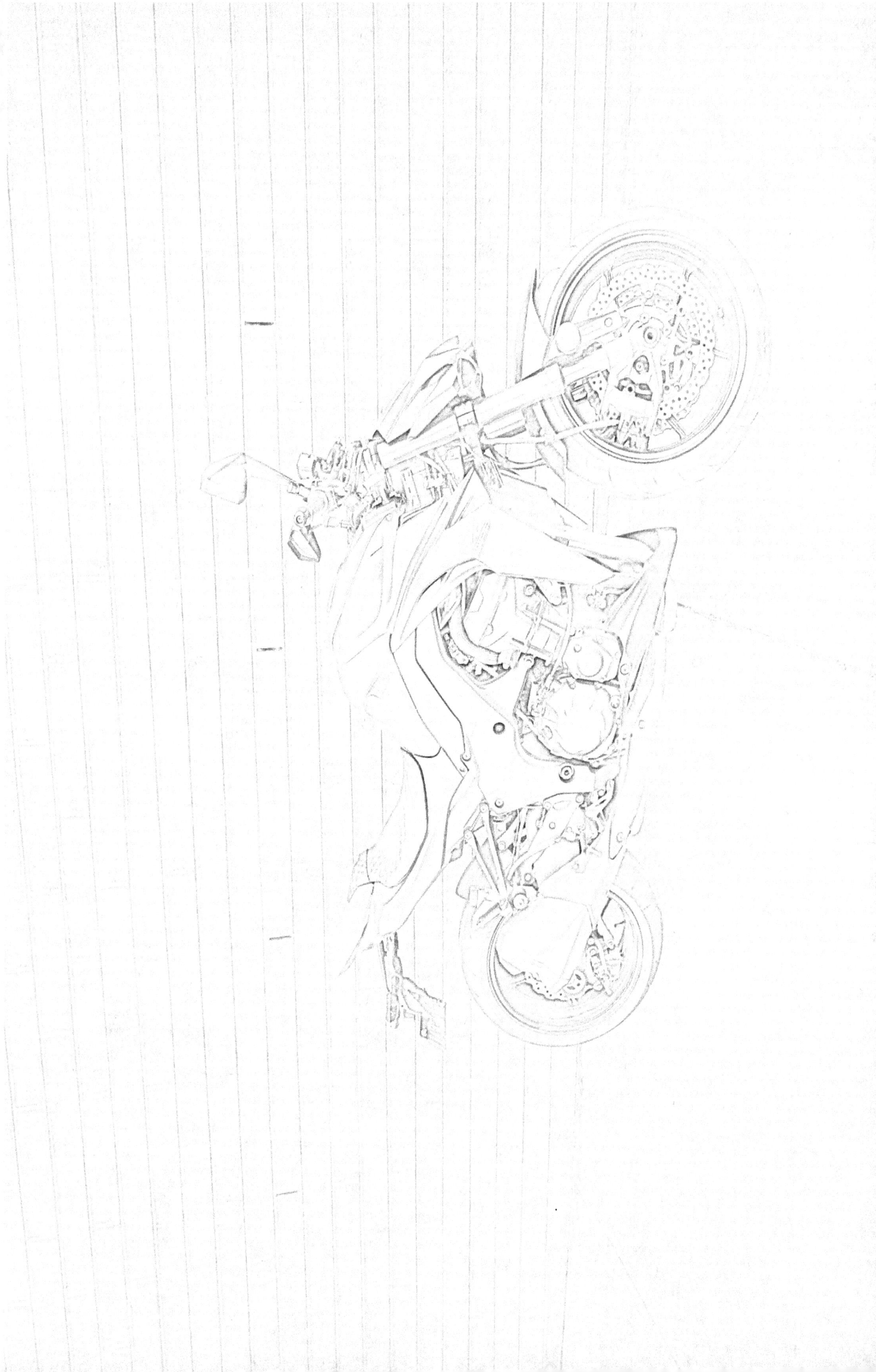

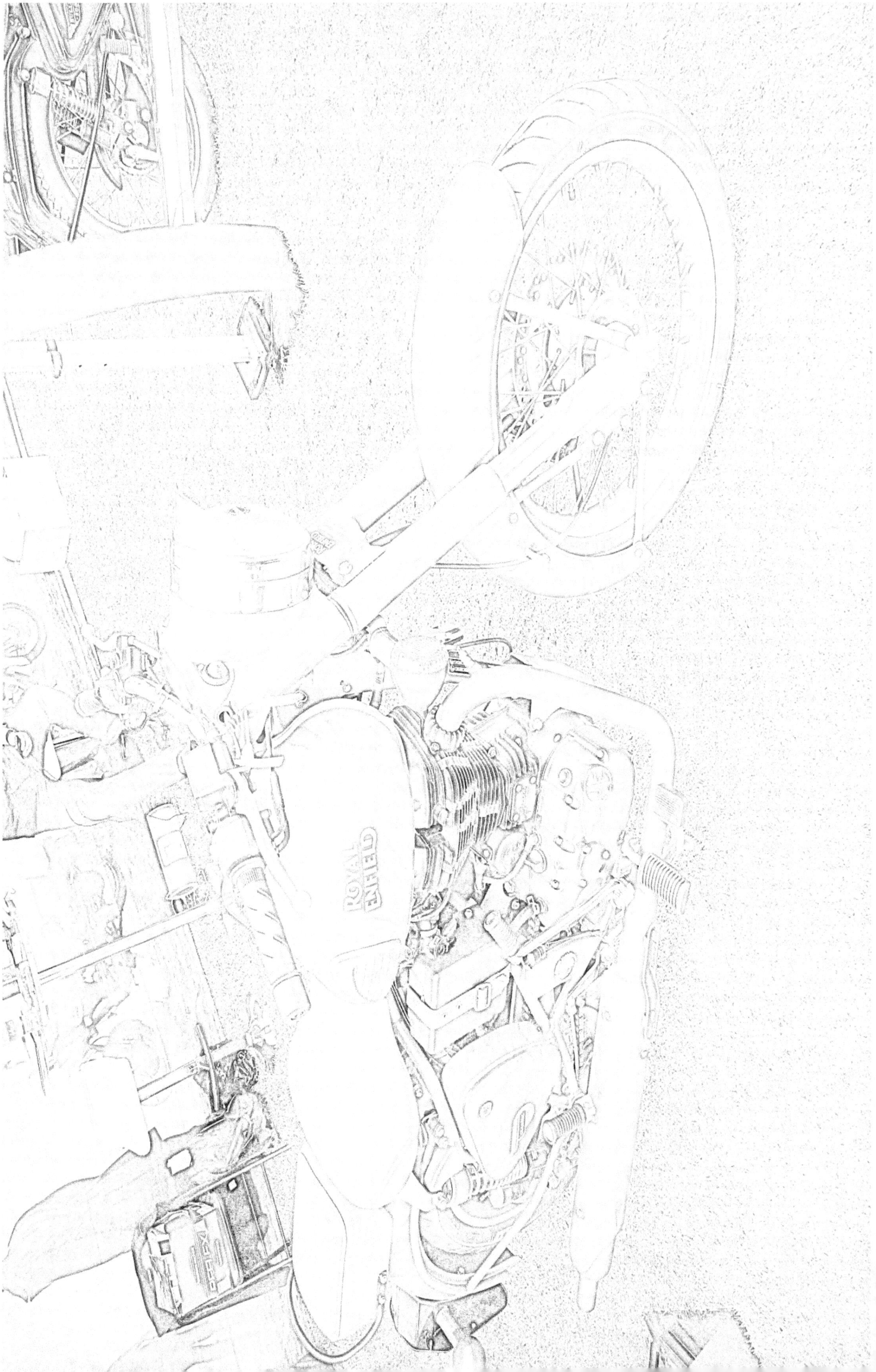
ROYAL
ENFIELD

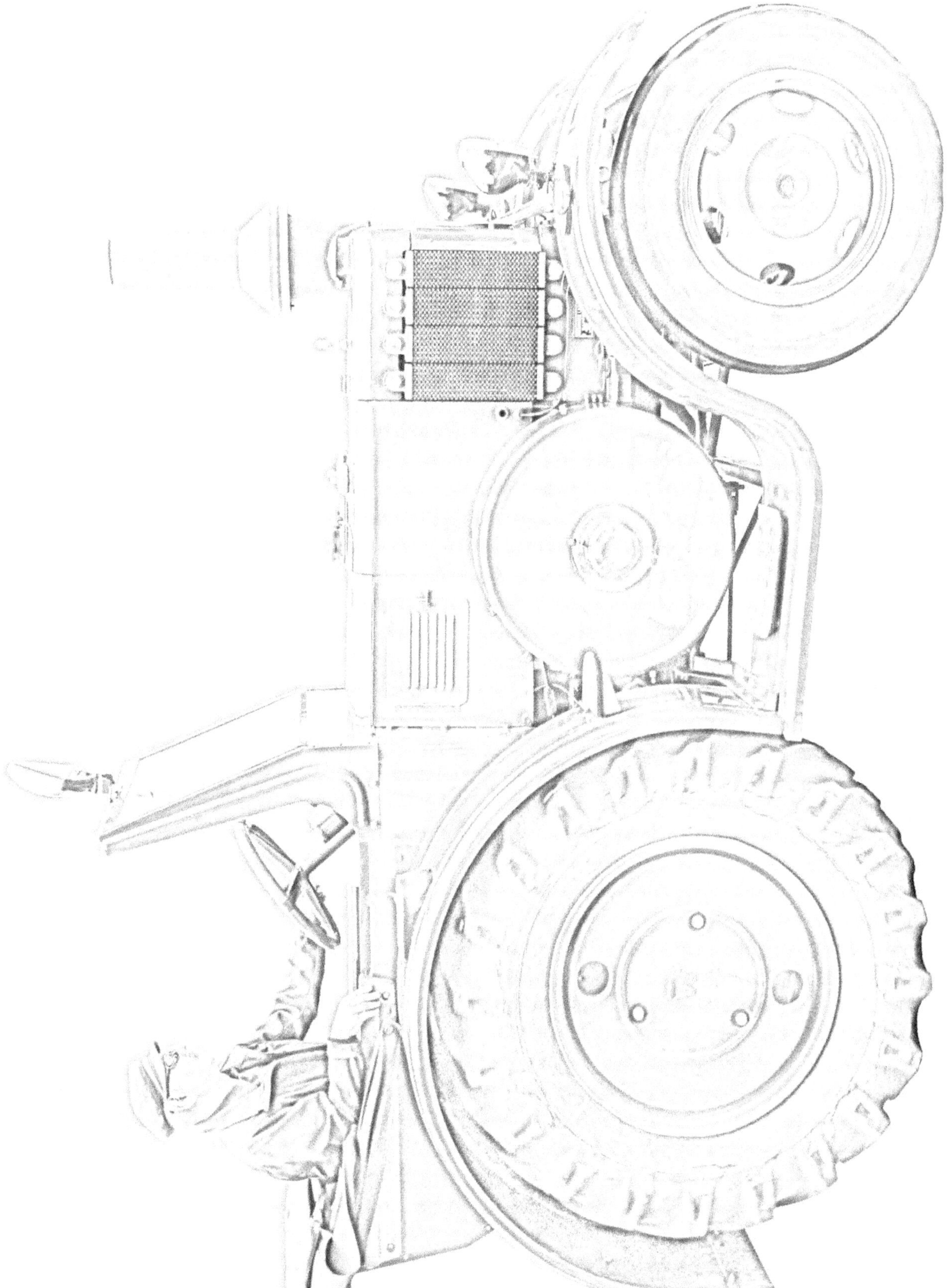

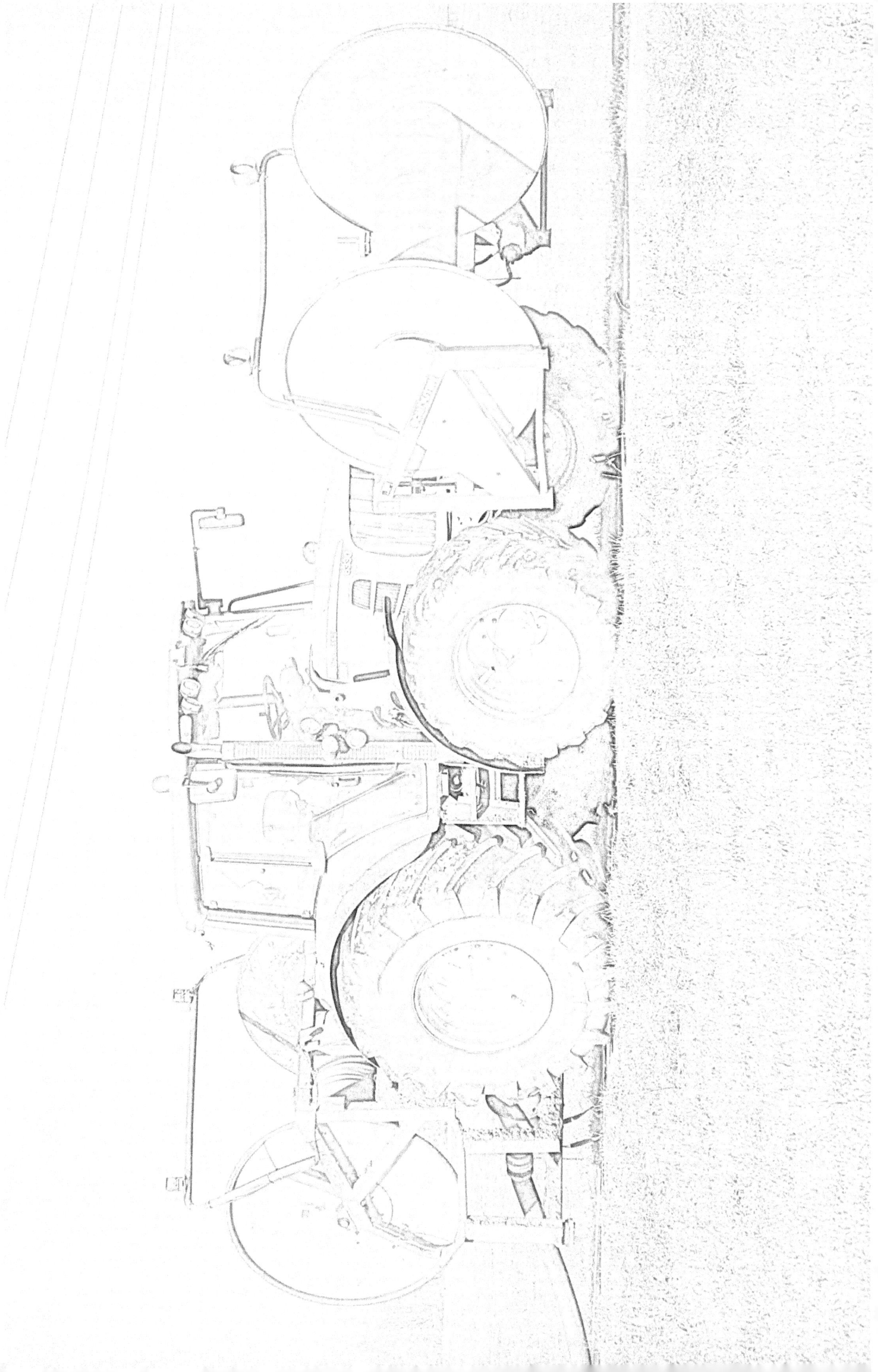

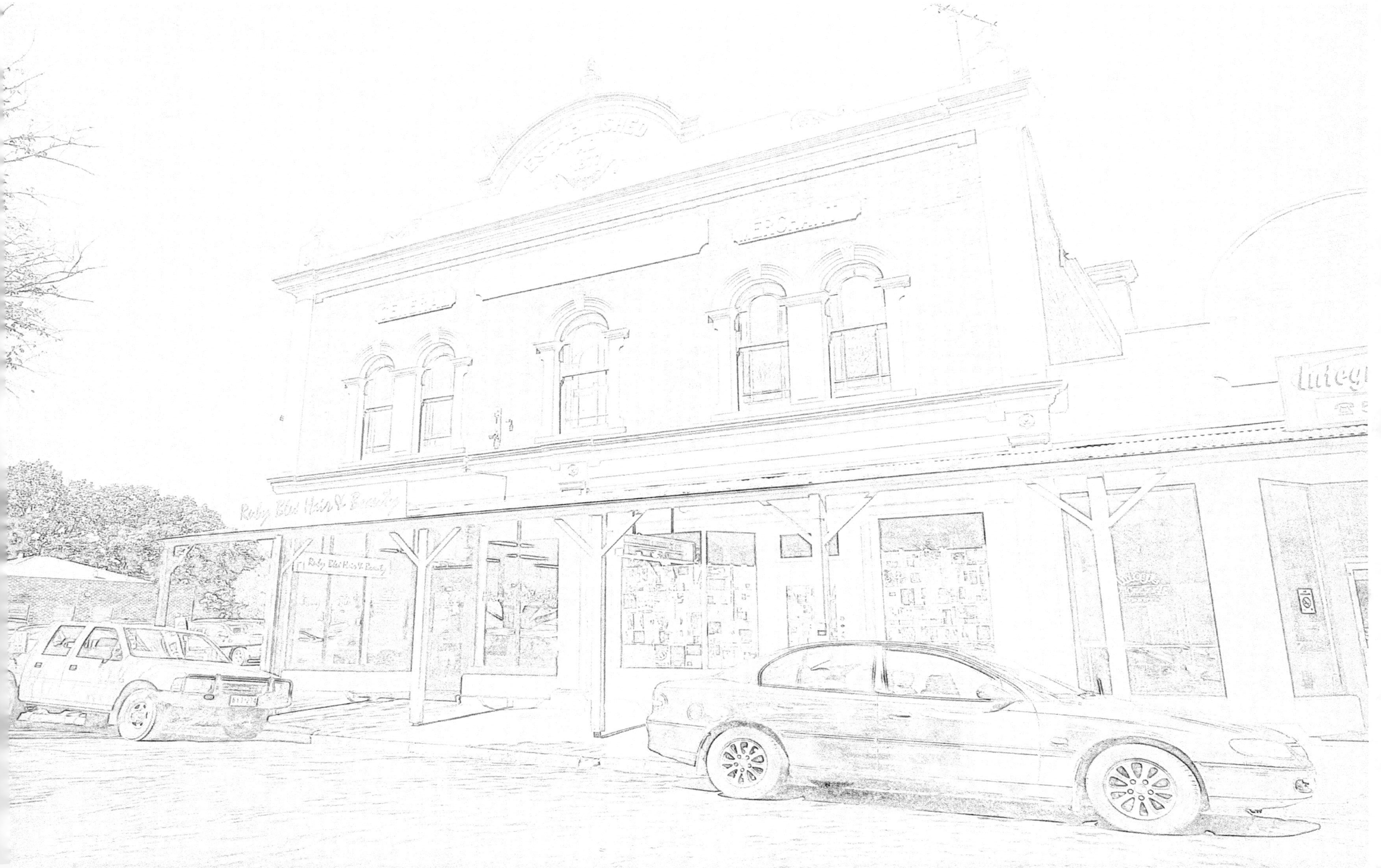
ESTABLISHED
MERCHANT
Ruby Blu Hair & Beauty

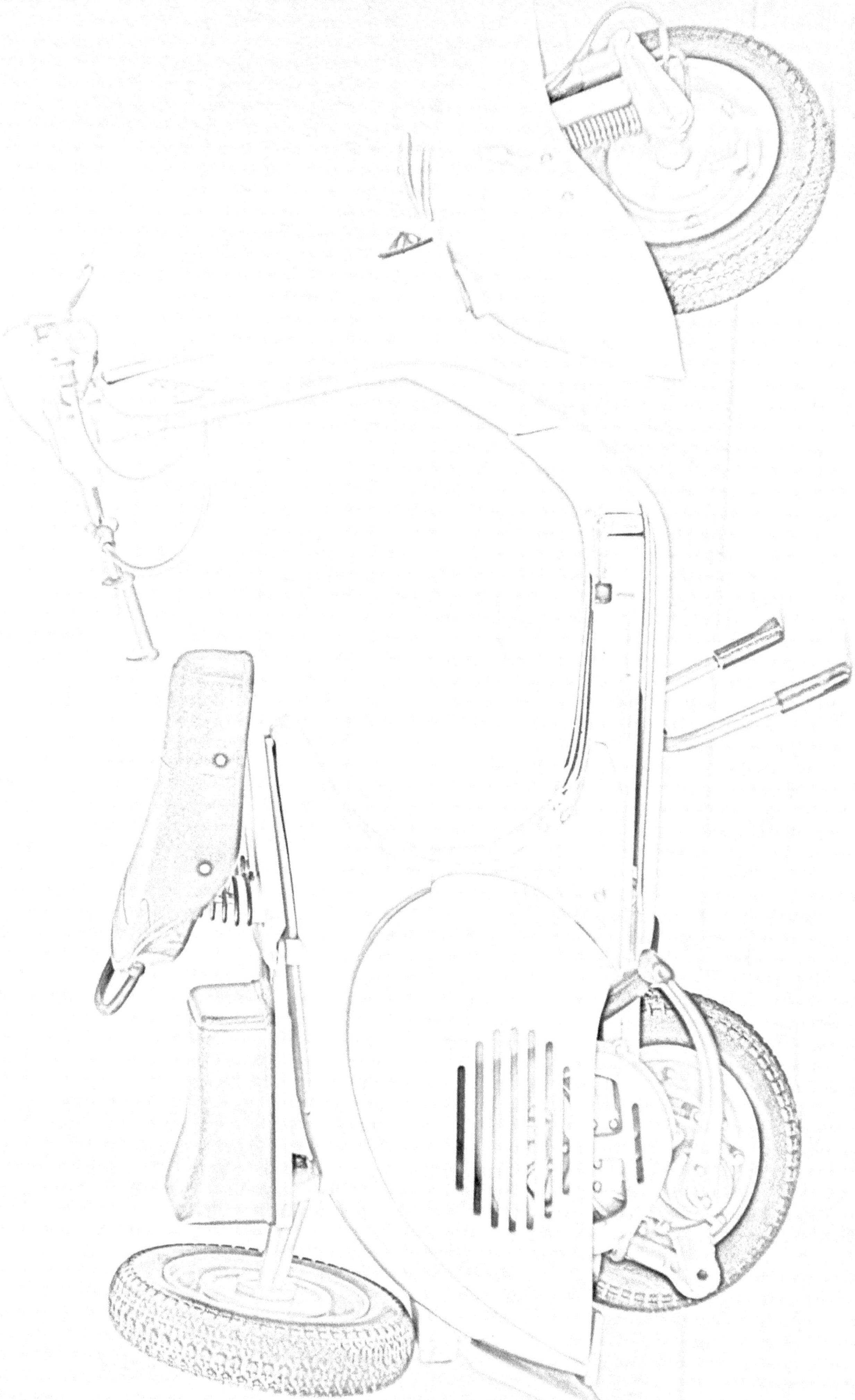

www.ingramcontent.com/pod-product-compliance
Lightning Source LLC
Chambersburg PA
CBHW081052180526
45170CB00005B/1766
* 9 7 8 0 3 5 9 8 3 2 8 4 2 *